LEARNING THROUGH PLAY
PROBLEM SOLVING

A Practical Guide for Teaching Young Children

By Ellen Booth Church

Illustrated by Nicole Rubel

Early Childhood Division Vice President and Publisher

Helen Benham

Editorial Director

Julia Kristeller

Editor

Ilene Rosen

Art Director

Mary Ann Salvato Jones

Designer

Rommel Alama

Production Editor

Katie Lyons

Senior Photo Researcher

Deborah Thompson

Published by:
Scholastic Inc.
Early Childhood Division
730 Broadway
New York, NY 10003

ISBN # 0-590-49485-6

12, 11, 10, 9, 8, 7, 6, 5, 4, 3, 2, 1   3, 4, 5, 6, 7, 8, /9
33

Printed in the U.S.A.
First Scholastic Printing, August 1993

CONTENTS

LEARNING AND GROWING WITH PROBLEM SOLVING

**Cover photo by
Richard Hutchings/PhotoEdit**

ACTIVITY PLANS
FOR TWOS, THREES, FOURS, AND FIVES

For Dr. Lois K. Nichols, my first mentor, who taught me how to
ask questions and inspire thinking.
And to the children of the van den Berg Learning Center, New Paltz,
New York, who challenged all I thought I knew.
— *Ellen Booth Church*

"When I think, ideas dance in my head!"

Hakim, age 4
van den Berg Learning Center
New Paltz, New York

FOREWORD:

A Conversation With Barbara Bowman

Barbara, we've been hearing a lot about problem solving. Why is it important to encourage young children to problem-solve?

All children in every culture are always solving problems. So in a way, it's not accurate to say we *want* children to problem-solve. They do it whether we want them to or not. What we can say is that we want to give children opportunities to solve many different types of problems and learn to value all kinds of thinking.

For many people, problem solving brings to mind the "word problems" we used to do in school. Has the meaning changed?

The definition has become much broader as researchers think more clearly about what problem solving means. We used to think problem solving was a particular kind of thinking that happened only in the domains of science and mathematics. We now know that many human activities, including art, social interaction, and physical movement, require problem solving as well.

The ways people solve problems look very different from one another. A mathematician may do most of his or her work manipulating ideas inside her head. Athletes and artists problem-solve more actively, using their bodies, equipment, and materials. But all of these people are thinking and solving problems and making valuable contributions to the culture.

As educators, we need to continually expose children to all different ways of solving problems.

Then later, when they reach high school or college, they can begin to specialize in one area of thinking — the one they enjoy most or do best.

Could you please talk more about culture and its relationship to problem solving?

Every culture needs people who can solve all types of problems. But most cultures tend to value certain types of problem solving over others. For example, the culture we live in places a high value on the sequential, step-by-step problem solving that is used in technology. Other cultures, however, might prefer different types of problem solving, such as social or artistic. Also, our culture tends to value people working individually, approaching problem solving in unique ways. Other cultures might prefer people to solve problems cooperatively and in more expected, accepted ways. Of course, there are differences within cultures as well, particularly in a culture as diverse as ours.

What do cultural preferences mean for teachers of young children?

The important point to remember is that while cultures may value some types of problem solving more highly, they still put some value on all types. We all want to be able to do a little of everything — enjoying sports, being empathetic, using technology, appreciating aesthetics, etc.

Teachers can help children learn to value all problem solving by offering a rich curriculum, asking many, many open-ended questions, and reflecting aloud on their own thinking and the thinking of others. But perhaps the most important way they can help is to be models. When children see that adults around them value creative, social, and physical expression and achievements as much as cognitive development, they will learn to value these achievements as well.

Barbara Bowman has been an early childhood teacher, consultant, author, and advocate for more than 40 years. She is currently the Director for Programs at the Erikson Institute of Loyola University in Chicago, Illinois.

PROBLEM SOLVING:
An Approach to Life

Problem solving is the process of identifying a problem or something you want to accomplish, thinking of ways to solve it, and trying out your ideas. It's something we all do every day. As adults, we're always trying to solve large and small problems, everything from career and family issues to what to do when the keys are locked inside the car. Children, too, constantly solve problems that arise in their play and throughout the day. As children interact with people and use materials, they set their own goals and test out solutions.

It's easy for us to take the ability to solve problems for granted, because it's such a part of life. But problem solving, like any skill, takes practice.

An early childhood setting is the perfect place to foster problem-solving abilities. When you create a place where children are encouraged to try to solve problems in their own ways, you let them know their ideas count and also help them learn new concepts. In the process, you help children build self-esteem and the confident sense that they have some control over their world.

Problem Solving Is a Way of Thinking

Problem solving is an ability that children use throughout their play. Children use problem solving when they experiment with and investigate things in their world, such as how far water will squirt

SUSAN RICHMAN

from a sprayer or what is inside a seed pod. They use problem solving when they select materials for building or to symbolize objects in their play. And they use problem solving when they are resolving an argument over a toy, or when a group tries to work together. While educators usually divide young children's learning into emotional, social, creative, cognitive, and physical development, problem solving crosses through all of these.

Why is this one skill important to so many kinds of activities? It's because problem solving is really a process of thinking that includes two other powerful skills — creative and critical thinking.

Creative thinking is the heart of problem solving. It is the ability to see a different way of doing something, create new ideas, and use materials in new ways. Being creative means being willing to take risks and develop something out of the ordinary. Creativity makes life and learning meaningful and fun.

Fluent and flexible thinking are parts of creativity. *Fluent thinking* is the ability to generate or "brainstorm" ideas. It can happen when children are working with thoughts or hands-on with materials. Thinking of all the different ways to get to school and naming everything you can think of that is blue are examples of fluent thinking.

Flexible thinking is the ability to see many possibilities, or view objects or situations in different ways. Children are masters at flexible thinking. They use it when they turn a pot into a hat or a spoon into a microphone, or when they think of many reasons why a child in a picture might feel sad.

Critical thinking is the ability to mentally break a whole problem or idea into parts. By looking first at the pieces, the larger problem becomes easier to understand and to solve. Sorting, classifying, analyzing, and comparing similarities and differences are critical-thinking activities common in early childhood programs. For example, when children compare containers filled with sand and analyze which one holds more, they are practicing critical thinking.

Asking questions about things that don't seem to make sense is another way children think critically. They use this ability naturally as they try to understand the things and relationships in their world. Questions such as, "Why do I have a shad-

ow on the playground but not inside?" or, "Why can't I see the wind?" are examples of critical thinking.

Following the Child's Lead

One of the best things about problem solving is that it's already happening in your room. Children solve problems naturally as they play. They make up their minds what they want to do — whether it's building a spaceship, pretending to be a butterfly, or exploring what a bullfrog does. Then they experiment with ways to do it. In this way, children are innately creative and critical thinkers. As you spend time with children, you can see their sense of curiosity and their problem-solving nature.

You foster problem solving in your program not so much through special materials or activities, but through your responsive, accepting attitude. When you provide plenty of time for free, open-ended play every day, you create opportunities for children to identify and solve problems. Then, when you follow their leads during play, you support their problem-solving efforts and help them accomplish their goals. And by celebrating children's original solutions, you let them know their ideas and efforts are valued.

At the same time, you can help extend children's creative thinking and problem solving by asking open-ended questions about their activities. In this way, you help them see the problem they are trying to solve in new and different ways. And by introducing activities that are based on children's interests and appropriate for their developmental levels, you can provide children with new challenges to meet and solve.

Developing the Whole Child

You know that problem solving is happening all the time. But why is it so important to encourage? One reason is that problem solving is an essential skill for life. In our fast-paced world, the only constant we can be sure about is change. It is impossible to predict what children will need to know or what problems they will face in the future. To thrive in this kind of world, people will need to be able to think on their feet, to create new ways of dealing with ideas and information — to constantly solve changing problems. This ability is perhaps the most important resource we can help children develop.

Problem solving influences every area of development — emotional, social, creative, cognitive, and physical. By being aware of and encouraging children's problem solving, you support development in each of these areas. And, at the same time, you help the whole child learn in natural, integrated ways.

Emotional Development

Solving problems helps children feel independent and builds their self-esteem. When children solve problems for themselves, they learn that they are competent, capable people who can impact their world in positive ways. This is especially important because, frequently in children's lives, adults seem to have all the answers and children are expected to follow directions. Such interactions can transmit such a negative message: "You don't know how to solve problems. Ask me, I have the answers."

Instead, the goal of early childhood programs is to empower children by offering a safe, supportive atmosphere to practice problem solving.

Social Development

One aspect of problem solving, sometimes called conflict resolution, is finding ways to settle disputes that arise between people. As you know, these are

Steps to Problem Solving

Problem solving is the process of identifying a problem or goal, generating ideas to solve it or reach it, then testing out ideas. The following steps are guidelines to help make this process happen. Not every problem follows these steps exactly, or has a definite solution. But by being aware of these steps, you can encourage and assist children as they solve the problems they meet during their play.

1. DEFINE THE PROBLEM

The first step in solving any problem is identifying what it is. Young children may not always recognize specific problems. They may feel frustrated or know that "something isn't working right," but not understand the cause. By asking open-ended questions that encourage children to talk about what they are doing, you help children identify problems.

Remember: Many young children might have trouble verbalizing what they think is happening. Help by providing words. You might say, "I see you're working hard on your puzzle, but that piece doesn't seem to fit in that place. Is there another place you could try?"

2. BRAINSTORM SOLUTIONS

Instead of immediately deciding on solutions, it is important for children to think of several options. Invite them to go beyond their first ideas by asking questions such as, "What's another way you can do this?" or, "What would happen if we tried a different way?" In this way, you invite children to expand their thinking.

Remember: Brainstorming is the time to think of — not evaluate — many possible solutions. Let children know that you welcome all their ideas, even if they don't make sense or seem a little crazy. To do this, accept every idea equally. Make sure you don't respond enthusiastically to a few ideas and mildly to others.

3. DECIDE WHERE TO START

After brainstorming, children choose which ideas to test out first. Be sure to let them take the lead. For individual projects, each child can make his or her own selection. For group projects, everyone can make the decision together.

Remember: Problem solving is very much a fluid process. Children might think of one thing to try, then reshape it, modify it, or abandon it to try something new. Let the process flow. It isn't necessary or even useful to encourage children to "stick to their plan."

among the most common problems children face. Cries of, "That's mine!" "I had it first!" and, "She won't play with me!" punctuate early childhood programs. By helping children apply problem-solving techniques to these situations, you help them learn an essential coping skill they can use for a lifetime.

Creative Development

Creativity — the ability to see things in different ways and brainstorm many solutions — is at the core of the problem-solving process. When children solve problems, their natural tendency to express themselves and their ideas is engaged. When you see children "mess around" with finger paint on a tray to find out what happens when the colors mix, or talk about how they will use blocks to build a spaceship, you are seeing active, creative problem solving. Ideas flow, children's imaginations are engaged, and thinking takes flight.

4. SELECT OR CREATE TOOLS

Help children think about what they will need to try out their solutions. Let them know they are free to use materials in your room in usual or unconventional ways. For example, fabric scraps might be good tools for making a collage, and also for plugging a hole in a water tube. For problems that are conflicts between people, remind children that words are the best tools.

Remember: Make sure materials in your room are easily accessible, so children can find and use them without asking for assistance. Be available to help them use words to express their feelings and find solutions during conflicts.

5. TEST AND ANALYZE SOLUTIONS

The final step is testing out solutions. Create a climate in your room that promotes hands-on experimentation — even if it sometimes means a mess, or if you believe an idea won't work. The learning and sense of independence children gain from trying are well worth the effort.

Remember: It is essential for children to know from the beginning that problem solving is more about process than about having correct solutions. Let them know you celebrate all their experiments. When solutions don't work, show your complete acceptance. Be supportive if children want to try again another way.

SUSAN WOOG WAGNER/PHOTO RESEARCHERS

Cognitive Development

Thinking critically, testing ideas, and analyzing results are all high-level thinking skills — and parts of problem solving. By solving problems, every child gets opportunities to practice these skills at his or her own developmental level. Also, solving problems leads to learning as children gain concepts in meaningful, hands-on ways. For example, when a child figures out how many blocks she needs to make a bridge, she not only solves the problem at hand. She also gains information about number and construction that she can use in the future.

Physical Development

Many of the problems children solve are physical in nature. This is true for all children, but especially for the very young. An infant learns through problem solving how to engage a parent with a smile, a coo, or a shake of a toy. A toddler learns through problem solving how to crawl under the table or stand up by holding the chair. A three-year-old learns through problem solving how to continuously roll a ball through a hoop. And four- and five-year-olds continue to use problem solving as they learn to climb, ride a tricycle, or toss a ball. When children solve physical problems, they use their bodies and their minds.

Problem Solving Is a Way to Have Fun

There's one other thing to remember about problem solving — enjoy it! When you encourage children to problem-solve on their own, you invite surprises into your room. No one knows exactly what will happen as long as problem solving is part of your day! By making room for spontaneous play and problem solving, you make learning interesting and exciting for children — and for you.

YOUR ROLE

Instead of being an instructor or teacher, your role in fostering problem solving is one of observer, supporter, facilitator, and model. As you become aware of the problem solving happening in your room, you'll find that there are times to watch children, times to encourage them, times to interact as a partner, and other times to show how you solve problems. Like the act of problem solving, your role is always changing.

Your Role as Observer

When you decided to work with young children, how did you see your role? What were the models for teaching that you had? For many of us, our school experiences showed us that a teacher is someone who provides information and directs children's activities. Yet observing — standing back and watching — can be one of the most important parts of your role. Through observation, you can learn to see, understand, and respect children's thinking.

Watch children's independent problem solving. Patience is an important attribute to develop in your role as observer. Sometimes it would be easier and faster to jump in and solve a problem for children, or show them the "right" way to do something. But stepping in too early can block children's own thinking. It can send them a message that you don't trust them to think problems through by themselves. Instead of intervening right away, relax and watch children's problem-solving processes unfold.

Learn to recognize problem solving. At first glance, children's problem solving doesn't always look like a thinking activity. Sometimes it can look like a fight, a rather risky experiment with objects, or an unusual — and messy — way to use art materials. Instead of viewing these events as problems for you, look for the thinking process that children are engaged in. Try to allow enough leeway for them to complete the problem-solving task. Remember that rules are important, but it's appropriate to bend them to meet children's needs at times — as long as nobody is going to get hurt.

Your Role as Supporter

When you support children's problem-solving efforts, you acknowledge the process in which they are involved and affirm that they are capable of handling problems. Through your support, you offer encouragement and let children know that what they are doing is important.

Acknowledge children's efforts. You might offer support by saying, for example, "Look at all the different ways you're trying to make that piece fit in your puzzle. You're working hard to figure it out, aren't you?" At other times, nonverbal support may be all that's needed. When you give a smile, an understanding nod, or a thumbs-up, you show support and encourage children to continue their thinking process. Just by sitting quietly next to a child, you can communicate: "I understand what you're doing, I know it's important, and I'm here to witness it."

Create an accepting environment. You set a supportive tone when you welcome children's original ideas, accept their contributions equally, and, at the same time, remain sensitive to their individual abilities and interests. In this atmosphere, children can feel free to express their ideas without fear of being wrong, or of not being taken seriously. Your setting becomes a protective "laboratory" where they can experiment and practice the problem-solving skills they'll use throughout their lives.

Promote open-ended play. Most problem solving occurs when children direct their own activities. That's why scheduling long periods of free play is so important. It gives children plenty of time to test out many possible solutions. Open-ended materials (objects that don't have a predetermined use) also create opportunities for children to initiate and solve their own problems. Include a wide variety of items such as cardboard boxes, tubes, and other "recycled treasures" in your environment.

Your Role as Facilitator

Problem-solving facilitators watch for times when children are engaged in their own problem solving, then interject provocative questions that propel children into new ways of thinking. The types of questions you ask have a strong influence. Open-ended, divergent questions that have many possible answers invite children to think and problem-solve. Closed-ended, convergent questions — those with right and wrong answers — can actually block children's thinking processes. (See "What Makes a Good Question?" page 12, for more information.) Facilitators don't offer solutions, but present sparks that encourage thought and creativity.

Encourage children to talk more. Who talks more in your room, you or children? Consider tape-recording a group-time session to find out. Play

Levels of Thinking

Bloom's Taxonomy [*Taxonomy of Educational Objectives*, Benjamin S. Bloom, editor (Longman)] explains that the process we call thinking really consists of several levels. Infants and toddlers use primarily the first two levels, but by age three, most children can use all six. By asking specific kinds of questions, you can help children experience and practice thinking on each of these levels.

Gathering knowledge means acquiring basic pieces of information. Questions at this level ask children to identify or describe objects. You might say, "I see you're using lots of materials in the water. What can you tell me about them?"

Comprehending and confirming looks at the meaning of the information gathered. You might say, "The yellow sponge floats. What about the other sponges? Do they float, too?"

Applying requires children to take what they've learned and use it in new situations. You might ask, "What can you make that will float using these materials?"

Analyzing is thinking about a whole in terms of its parts. You might ask, "Which material do you think will be best to start your boat? A wood piece? A foam tray?"

Synthesizing asks children to put parts together to form a whole. You might ask, "How can we use all the materials together to make a boat?"

Evaluating includes comparing and making judgments. You might ask, "Which materials worked best? Why?"

What Makes a Good Question?

Asking questions is at the heart of your role in encouraging problem solving. But not every question promotes good problem-solving thinking.

Convergent or closed-ended questions such as, "What color is this?" or, "How many do you see?" can limit problem solving. Children either know the answers or they don't, and there's no room for offering their ideas or opinions. And, as you know, young children learn quickly how it feels to give an answer that's "wrong." Rather than take risks, many children learn not to answer at all.

Divergent or open-ended questions, however, such as, "What do you think?" or, "What should we try?" have no right or wrong answers. They allow children to take risks and experiment with their ideas. As a result, children are much more likely to use and develop problem-solving skills. Divergent questions also enhance language skills, because children usually need phrases and sentences to communicate their thoughts, instead of simply answering in one or two words.

How to Ask Good Questions

Making sure you ask children questions that promote problem solving whenever possible requires self-assessment and practice. Here are tips to keep in mind when you formulate and ask questions.

Pay attention to the ways you begin your questions. "How do you think we could …?" and, "How many ways can you …?" are good ways to begin divergent questions. Convergent questions tend to begin with words like *do, did, are,* and *is.*

Ask children the kinds of open-ended questions they often ask adults. How do you answer when children ask, "Why is the sky blue?" "Why do the leaves change colors?" Why not ask them what they think? With young children, it's more important to encourage creative thinking than to immediately provide accurate, yet often complex or incomplete, answers.

Ask divergent questions in various situations. Some questions encourage children to brainstorm many possibilities: "What are all the ways we can use the wrapping paper Cara's mom brought in?" Others ask them to figure out solutions: "I found this puzzle piece on the floor. How can we find out where it belongs?"

Accept everyone's answers equally. Although one child's response might excite you more than others, it's important for children to see and feel that their ideas are not being judged.

Encourage children to elaborate on their ideas. Sometimes children may need your help to keep open-ended conversations going. If they seem "stuck," try posing additional divergent questions based on their previous comments and responses. For example, you might ask, "What else can you tell me about it?" "What do you think would happen next?" Help children learn to respond to one another and ask their own questions.

Record children's thoughts on paper. You validate children's ideas when you write them down (whether children can read them or not). Record their ideas often on experience charts, then post the charts in your room. By doing this, you encourage children to continue thinking, expressing, and trying out their ideas.

back the tape and listen for the percentage of "teacher talk" versus "child talk." Then look for ways to increase children's participation even more.

For example, try this method. Suppose you want to talk about the art activity that's available today. Instead of telling children what they can make, show them the materials and invite them to brainstorm many possible ideas. You might say, "I need your help. I brought in this bag full of art materials. What do you think we can make with them?" Then act on children's ideas and allow them to make whatever they choose. You can offer your own suggestions as well. This is a very successful way to help children begin problem solving. When they see that you don't have one "right" answer in mind, they can move past their fears of being "wrong" and use their wonderfully creative thinking.

Provide a variety of problem-solving experiences.
As a facilitator, part of your role is to offer a range of experiences that allow children to practice problem solving in different ways. Games, puzzles, and discussions; art, science, and math projects that they help design; and literature all provide children with opportunities to stretch their minds.

Your Role as a Model
Whether or not you're aware of it, children are always watching you. As they observe the ways you deal with problems, they see examples of ways they might solve problems themselves.

Think about your approach to problem solving.
What kind of problem solver are you? Do you enjoy tackling new problems? Do you tend to prefer solutions that are tried-and-true? The ways you experienced problem solving in school and at home when you were young probably affect your reaction. But whatever your feelings, it's important for children to see you addressing and solving problems.

Talk about problem solving.
When problems arise in your room, discuss your thought processes as you solve them. For example, you might say, "I have a problem. I planned to put out finger painting today, but we ran out of finger-paint paper. Should we use different paper? Or wait until tomorrow, and I'll buy more tonight? Maybe I'll ask Mrs. Fairfield in the threes room if we can borrow some of hers." This way, you model an attitude as well as a process for solving the small problems that are part of everyday life. (You can involve children further by asking them to suggest their own solutions to the problem.) Also, when you emphasize words such as *problem*, *think*, *ideas*, and *solve*, children begin to use them to describe their own thinking.

Be willing to make mistakes.
Jean Piaget once said, "The process of learning is the process of making mistakes." Let children see some of the mistakes you make, then ask them to help you solve the resulting problem. There is nothing more freeing for children than discovering that adults can make mistakes, too. They feel important when they help you, and, at the same time, they find out that making mistakes isn't really such a "bad" thing, after all. Instead, it's an opportunity for learning.

AGES & STAGES
of Problem-Solving Development

The way children engage in problem-solving activities depends not only on their experiences, but also on their ages and developmental levels. Use these guidelines as you think about problem solving to help determine the various abilities and interests in your group.

TWO-YEAR OLDS MAY:

■ create new uses for toys and materials in totally unexpected ways, such as filling a hat like a purse or using applesauce for finger paint.

■ experiment with the same problem over and over again, such as stacking up a block tower that keeps falling down.

■ test their physical problem-solving skills by climbing over chairs instead of going around them or sliding down the stairs on their bottoms.

■ produce a wonderful mess in the process of problem solving.

■ want to be helpful and enjoy finding ways to fix things.

You can help by:

■ creating a safe environment where children are encouraged to experiment.

■ allowing twos to keep trying to find solutions without solving the problems for them or offering "right" answers too quickly.

■ supporting their creative problem solving by using comments such as, "What a great new way to use that material!"

■ accepting that independent eating and cleaning up are important problem-solving activities, and that messes are part of the process.

■ remembering that even though every object in your room has a place, it doesn't always have to be *in* its place. When twos use toys in different places and ways, they are problem solving.

THREE-YEAR-OLDS MAY:

■ experiment with materials in slightly more creative and detailed ways than twos, such as using toy bananas as telephones or pots as hats.

■ use language in their problem solving.

■ delight in showing you their thinking. They may repeatedly demonstrate their clever new inventions and ideas.

■ try to "make" something work when they are having difficulty. For example, they might try pounding puzzle pieces into places where they don't fit.

■ show curiosity about new things and be fascinated by exploring how they work.

You can help by:

■ providing a classroom filled with open-ended, undefined materials for children to use in new and creative ways.

■ listening to children's ideas and acknowledging their thinking in specific ways, such as, "You solved your problem! When you decided to put those blocks there, you kept the train from falling off the track."

■ being supportive when they are frustrated, but avoiding solving their problems for them.

■ sparking their curiosity by bringing in new and unusual things to discuss and explore.

FOUR-YEAR-OLDS MAY:

■ construct elaborate ways to solve problems. Fours not only use objects to represent other things, they also add art and other materials to actually create new items.

■ experiment with problems of language by telling jokes and inventing new words.

■ begin to get very involved in solving social problems. Fours are highly concerned about rules and helping others find fair solutions.

■ enjoy experimenting and problem solving with ideas as well as concrete materials. Questions like, "What will happen if …?" or, "What might happen next?" naturally arise as fours begin to imagine new situations.

You can help by:

■ providing a rich, varied collection full of raw materials, including art and fastening materials, so children can experiment, construct, and create.

■ supporting their experiments with humor and language. Laugh with their jokes. Acknowledge new words they create and the thinking they use to create them.

■ being available to help children solve social problems without solving them yourself. Asking, "What's the problem here?" or, "What are you going to do now?" may be enough to get children talking and attacking the problem — instead of one another.

■ stimulating creative problem solving by asking children to predict what they will see when they go for a walk, or what would happen if a dragon came into your room.

■ reading books that encourage children to solve problems or predict outcomes in the story. (See "Good Books for Problem Solving," page 23, for suggestions.)

FIVE-YEAR-OLDS MAY:

■ enjoy tackling bigger problems of construction than threes and fours. For example, children might create a digging machine for the sandbox by combining existing items with art and construction materials.

■ show a new level of frustration when they can't solve complex problems as quickly as they used to solve easier ones.

■ be more adept at problem solving using ideas. They often consider and discuss how possible solutions might work before trying them out.

■ enjoy creative thinking games, such as brainstorming all the ways they can use or do something. Some fives enjoy making up games for others to try.

■ be very verbal when they talk about problem solving. Fives are beginning to be able to explain their thinking and delight in telling you in detail about their ideas.

You can help by:

■ creating a rich, supportive environment in which fives can problem-solve using both objects and ideas. In addition to an excellent collection of materials, provide interesting pictures and books that invite children to think creatively and problem-solve.

■ showing you understand their frustrations while supporting them as they solve their problems. Help children regain their focus by asking open-ended questions.

■ making certain that children feel safe in your program to experiment and take risks, without fear of "failure."

■ offering many ideas and opportunities for brainstorming that follow children's interests.

■ asking open-ended questions instead of giving information. (See "What Makes a Good Question?" page 12, for more information.)

WHAT DO YOU DO WHEN...

In the day-to-day interactions among children, adults, and materials, problems to solve arise naturally. Children solve problems when they match cards in a lotto game, settle a dispute over a toy, learn to climb the ladder to the slide, or find a new way to build a sculpture using recycled materials. Often, children encounter and solve these problems independently. But at other times, you can help facilitate and enhance their efforts. Following are six examples of situations in which an adult can help foster problem solving, along with suggestions for ways to respond to each one. Of course, there is no one right way to help children problem-solve, just as there is no one right way for children to solve problems themselves. These examples simply offer guidelines you can use to help effectively support and facilitate children's problem solving.

"I WONDER WHAT THIS IS?"

It's the first sunny day after several days of hard rain, and the children are eagerly rediscovering the playground. As they play near some of the older metal equipment, Denise stops. "Look at this orange stuff on the climber bars," she says. "What is it?" A few more children gather around and also wonder what the "orange stuff" can be. Osel says, "Maybe it's a kind of paint somebody put on."

Here's a way to help: The children are excited about their discovery, but they may need help to extend their interest and answer their questions. This event is a wonderful opportunity for predicting and hypothesizing. Instead of explaining what rust is, ask children to think about what this substance might be. Pose more questions to encourage investigation, such as, "What does the orange stuff look like to you? Did you ever see anything like it before? Where?" Then, to help children learn more and expand their thinking, you might suggest that they search the playground for more rust. Talk

together about the places where they find rust and see if there are any similarities.

If children remain interested, you can follow up their observations by suggesting experiments that encourage more problem solving. For example, invite children to select a variety of objects to drop in cups of water. Encourage children to predict if any of the items will rust, then test the results after a few days.

"THIS BOOK IS RUINED!"

Marcus and Jaleesa are enjoying books together in the library corner when they discover that one of them has many ripped pages. Upset, they run to you. "Look what somebody did to our book!" Jaleesa says. "That's bad. Now we have to throw it away."

Here's a way to help: Throwing the book away is one way to solve this problem, but Jaleesa is not happy with it. By showing her and Marcus that there are other possibilities, you empower them — and also help them learn the useful skill of fixing books. Begin by acknowledging feelings. You might say, "Ripped books upset me, too. But maybe we can find a way to save this one. What do you think we could do to fix it?" Invite the children to brainstorm different possibilities, and suggest that they look in the art area for materials they might use. Once they have generated ideas, encourage them to experiment and make the repairs themselves. Support their efforts to help them experience success.

Later, at group time, ask Marcus and Jaleesa to share what happened and how they solved the problem. Then extend the problem-solving experience by asking the group to brainstorm ways to prevent this from happening again. Invite children to offer ideas and possibly make up their own rules for looking at books. Write their suggestions on an experience chart for future reference.

"IT WON'T WORK!"

In the dramatic-play area, a few children are working together to create a car out of large boxes. One of their ideas is to use foil pie plates as headlights, but they are having trouble finding a way to attach the pie plates to the car. You observe as children problem-solve on their own. First they try using glue, then paste, but the plates keep falling off. Finally, a very frustrated Ami comes to you saying, "It won't work! We can't get the headlights to stay on and we tried everything!"

Here's a way to help: By asking a simple question to spark children's thinking, you can help them see new ways to solve their problem. You might ask, "Why do you think the plates won't stay on?" This way, you invite children to analyze the situation before they consider solutions. Then you might walk together to the art or woodworking area so children can see all the different materials that are available for fastening. Instead of handing them tape or brass fasteners, invite children to experiment with whatever materials they choose. Then step back, observe, and offer support as they tackle the problem again. Be sure to acknowledge all children's efforts — the ones that don't work as well as the ones that do.

"CAN YOU DO IT FOR ME?"

Lanie is sitting with a group at the drawing table. Many of the children are drawing pictures of themselves. Lanie tries, too, but he isn't as skilled at this kind of drawing as some of the other children. He becomes frustrated and unhappy. Finally, he turns to you. "I can't draw my face," he says. "Will you draw it for me?"

Here's a way to help: To express themselves creatively through art, children sometimes need to solve problems about materials or techniques. One way to help Lanie without solving his problem for him (and missing an opportunity to foster his self-esteem) is to encourage a step-by-step approach. Offer Lanie a mirror and, together, look at his reflection. Suggest that he look carefully at his face and think about its shapes. You might say, "What shapes do you see? What shape is your head? What shape are your eyes? Which shape could you draw first?" Offer more questions and suggestions to support him through the process.

Remember, too, that some children feel more comfortable and successful using materials other than markers or crayons. If Lanie prefers gluing to drawing, you might suggest that he use collage materials to represent his face. Clay and paint are other possible choices.

"IT'S MINE!"

Hakim and Beth are playing next to each other in the block corner. They are both building busily when, at the same time, they reach for the same block. Both children tug on the block and become angry. Not surprisingly, a battle begins. "It's my block!" "I had it first!" Each child is upset and clearly believes the block belongs to him or her.

Here's a way to help: It is important for children to take an active part in solving social conflicts. But first, they need help to control their emotions and define the problem. Hold the block while the children take a moment to calm down. Then ask each child, one at a time, to tell his or her version of the event while the other listens. Next, encourage them to think of solutions so they can both feel satisfied. Maybe there are similar blocks on the shelf that they can count out equally and share, or perhaps they can combine their blocks and build a larger structure together. Help Hakim and Beth choose one solution, then observe for a few moments as they return to their play.

"IT'S TOO NOISY IN HERE."

It's group time, and the discussion about the new storybook has gotten out of hand. It seems that everyone is talking at once! Finally a few children stop and hold their ears while others "shush" their friends to be quiet.

Here's a way to help: In this situation, you can choose to solve the problem yourself by telling everyone to be quiet. But children benefit

more when they are involved in finding a solution. Ask them to take the first step by identifying the problem. You might say, "We have a problem here. What's happening?" After a few children express their ideas, move on to the next step. You might ask, "How can we solve the problem of everybody talking at once?" Write down children's suggestions, being careful to accept all ideas equally. Next, think about materials that might help solve the problem. You might ask, "Could we use something to help us remember whose turn it is to talk?" Offer suggestions if needed, such as a marble or stone that children hold when it's their turn. Then, be sure to test out their solutions. Try the different ideas for a while, talk about which works best, and decide together which to adopt for your room.

Encouraging Problem-Solving Skills in Children With SPECIAL NEEDS

Encouraging children with special needs to acquire problem-solving skills offers a way toward greater self-reliance and more successful functioning throughout life. Learning problem-solving skills is especially important for children who will need to do lots of problem solving just to get along in their daily lives. For example, a person in a wheelchair is often confronted with obstacles such as curbs, stairs, gravel walks, and counters that are hard to reach. Well-meaning adults may tend to shelter children with disabilities by solving problems for them. But you can help children gain skills and self-esteem when you allow them to tackle manageable problems on their own.

Children learn best by interacting directly with their environment. Encourage children with special needs to take an active, physical role in problem solving. Remember, watching others is not enough. But active participation might require special physical arrangements for some children. Parents and therapists can often offer helpful suggestions. A child with limited vision might need bright indirect lighting to see best. A child with a physical disability might be able to control his or her arm and head best by lying on the floor, with her chest over a bolster and arms forward. It's very important to determine individual needs and make whatever physical adaptations are necessary so every child can experience success in problem solving.

To help a child learn problem-solving strategies, observe her for a while to discover ways that she solves problems most eagerly and easily. One blind child might ask lots of questions to figure out problem situations, while another blind child might work better alone, examining and experimenting with materials using her hands.

While each child is different, children with similar disabilities share some common needs. The following are suggestions for helping children with various disabilities acquire problem-solving skills.

Children With Hearing Disabilities

Most people "talk to themselves" mentally, or "self-talk" when they are thinking and solving problems. For example, they might think, If I put some clay in this hole, the boat will stop leaking. But children with hearing loss often develop language skills at a slower pace than other children, including the ability to "self-talk." As a result, children with hearing loss may not solve problems as efficiently as their peers. To help a child with a hearing disability put thought processes into language, first allow him or her to solve a problem independently. Then ask him to talk about the situation and explain how he solved the problem. You might say, "Dino, you fixed the truck. How did you make the wheels stay on?" It's important to allow plenty of time for the child to communicate his thoughts without anticipating what he wants to say and saying it for him. However, if the child doesn't have the vocabulary to explain a thought, this is a good opportunity to introduce new words. For example, you might say, "That thing is a paper clip. How did you use it?"

If you introduce a problem-solving activity, make sure the child hears your directions and explanations. Look directly at the child as you speak. Talk at a normal volume and speed without exaggerated lip movements. To ensure that the child understands you, ask specific clarifying ques-

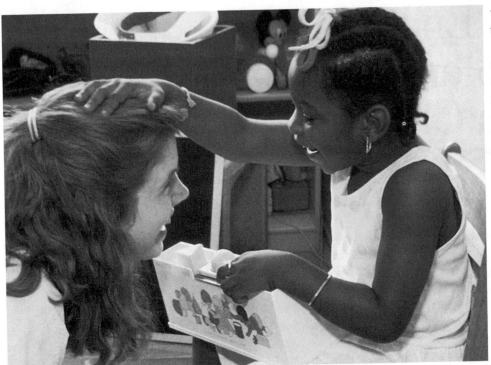

when to ask for help and when to do things independently.

A young child with a visual disability can become extremely frustrated when everyone else is aware of something that he or she is not, because she does not know that she experiences the world differently from others. She might not realize that others can see until she reaches five, six, or even seven years old. As a result, she may turn her frustration against herself and develop low self-esteem, or she may become angry when things just don't make sense. Gradually, she may give up on her own problem-solving abilities and simply turn to others for solutions. To help a child feel more positive about her own abilities, be reassuring and specific. You might say, "I know you feel bad because you can't see the puzzle like Jan can. If you try touching it with your fingers, you can solve it, too." Remarks should always refer to a specific situation, not become a general discussion of the child's condition. After many of these types of experiences, a child learns about her limitations and at the same time feels assured about her many abilities.

Children who will be learning braille need lots of opportunities during early childhood to develop fine-motor skills and extra sensitivity in their fingertips. You can set up problem-solving situations to promote these skills, such as asking a child to remove the lid from a jar, make a line with pegs on a pegboard, remove clothes from a doll, or find the correct key for unlocking a drawer.

tions such as, "What tools will you use?" Then observe the child from time to time as he does the activity.

Children With Visual Disabilities

Children learn a lot about problem solving by watching others solve problems and copying or adapting those techniques. Because they cannot learn by watching, children with visual disabilities generally require much more time and experience to learn how to solve problems. You can help by explaining how others solved a problem that is giving particular trouble. For example, you might invite the child to feel blocks on a shelf and say, "Tanya stacked the blocks on top of each other this way. Then they all fit on the shelf." It also helps for the child to work with other children. You might need to remind others to include the child in the activity at hand. This can become a problem-solving situation in itself when you ask, "How can Olivia help with the bridge?" or, "Olivia, how can you help with the bridge?"

While children with visual disabilities need more help than others in learning how to solve problems, learning to accept help requires maturity. During early childhood, a child might want to express independence — as most young children do — and refuse assistance. Or, a child might act overly dependent and want help with almost everything. Remember, it takes a long time for children with severe visual disabilities to learn

Children With Physical Disabilities

By using problem solving, a child with physical disabilities can find ways to actively engage in learning situations. Problem-solving strategies serve to make activities more inviting. For example, many children with physical disabilities may not like to touch messy materials such as paste, paint, sand, and cookie dough. For finger painting, you might provide sponges, paper towels, blunt pencils, and other tools and ask, "How can you use these to make paint marks?"

Children With Mental Retardation

Children with mental retardation often need lots of encouragement to get involved in problem solving.

You can promote problem solving by first serving as a model. If a child is near the blocks, you might stack three blocks, talking through the problem-solving process as the child watches. You might ask, "How could I make a tower with these blocks? I could put a block here and another block on top of it. Oh, it fell off! I'll try a small block instead. That one's staying on. Now I'll try another block." Then invite the child to complete the last step of the process by saying, "Try putting another block on the tower. Which one do you think will stay on?" Once a child successfully solves a problem, he or she might want to repeat it over and over. That's okay — it helps the child remember the concepts involved and feel a sense of accomplishment. However, children with mental retardation often repeat familiar actions over and over for the feeling of security it gives, even when they are cognitively ready to move on to the next step. Once a child masters a task, gently encourage him to try something a little bit more challenging. You might say, "You stacked the three blocks so well. Try doing stacking with these cans. Which one do you think would be best on the bottom?"

It is helpful for a child with mental retardation to play near other children who are somewhat more skilled at problem solving. The child can observe what they do and learn from them. Encourage the other children to talk to the child and include him in their play. You might say to them, "Tell Jerome how he can help you. He knows how to stack blocks, too."

Children With Emotional Disabilities

Children with emotional disabilities generally display one of three types of extreme behaviors: aggression, withdrawal, or hyperactivity. Problem solving is an excellent way for children with emotional disabilities to gain self-confidence and learn to attend to a task. It's important to make certain that the problem a child tackles is at his or her ability level. Too much challenge can lose the attention of a hyperactive child, trigger emotional outbursts in an aggressive child, or prompt further withdrawal in a withdrawn child.

Children who are extremely withdrawn often hesitate to become actively involved in learning situations. Introduce problem-solving materials that seem to spark a child's interest. You might notice the child looking at or standing near a particular material. Don't push the child. It can be more successful to model by using the materials as you describe what you're doing. You might say, "I want to make a hole in this paper. How could I make a hole?" If the child seems interested, you might ask for suggestions. If this makes the child withdraw more, simply complete the activity as you continue to talk about your actions. If the child does decide to join you, play together for a while and then gradually try to step away to promote independent problem solving.

Children who use aggressive behaviors need lots of praise for solving problems of any kind. Because they often have trouble solving problems calmly, they need assurance when they do. If an aggressive child does display extreme behavior in a problem-solving situation, help him calm down and then talk about the situation, asking him to suggest ways to solve the problem at hand. If possible, the child should get another chance to solve the problem using his own ideas.

Children who display hyperactive behaviors

experience the most success when problem-solving activities are short and interesting. Give the child lots of praise for keeping his attention focused and suggest another activity if he becomes restless. Children with hyperactive behaviors often experience periods when they are not as excitable. Watch for patterns of calm behavior, such as just after snack or first thing in the morning. At those times, you might introduce problem-solving activities that require concentration.

Problem solving makes learning about the world a fun experience and, at the same time, builds self-esteem, confidence, and the ability to take on challenges independently. These are all vital for children with disabilities.

Merle Karnes, Ed.D., is a professor of special education at the University of Illinois at Urbana-Champaign.

LAURA DWIGHT

ARRANGING YOUR SETTING

The way you arrange your setting has a strong effect on children's opportunities to problem-solve. If you strictly control how children use space and spend time, you limit their chances to make decisions and experiment with materials and ideas. But when children can choose and direct their own play, you invite them to use their minds and social skills to work out everyday problems.

Remember, too, that your interactions with children are the most important part of your setting. Whether you have a tiny space with just a few materials or a well-stocked, spacious room, it is your support and acceptance of children's individuality and thinking that make the biggest difference.

Organize for independence. A good problem-solving setting is more child-directed than teacher-directed. Children know the routines, choose their activities, and are active participants in creating rules. Plenty of open-ended materials are accessible in all areas of the room. They are clearly marked so children can find, use, and return them without teacher assistance. Each item has a "home base," or place where it belongs, but during free play children can use materials interchangeably throughout the room.

Create learning centers to foster social problem solving. It is much easier for children to practice negotiating and resolving conflicts with just a few other children. Use play furniture and storage shelves to organize your room into workable, welcoming learning centers. Think about traffic patterns and how children will move from one center to another, so that no one will be likely to run through and interrupt other children's play. Your goal is to limit conflicts caused by the environment so children can focus on problems that arise through play.

ERIKA STONE

Helping Problem Solving Come Alive in Every Play Setting

The ways you arrange space and materials within learning centers also influence problem solving. All areas of your setting, including the playground, should invite children to use creative, constructive, and social problem-solving skills. Use this discussion of key play areas to help you consider ways to enhance children's problem solving around your room and throughout your day.

Art Area
Art is a rich area for both creative and critical think-

ing. When children decide what to do about paint that's running down their picture or how to make a cotton ball stick to paper, they are involved in problem solving. By varying the materials in your art area, you can inspire children to think of new ways to create.

■ Vary the sizes, colors, shapes, and types of paper you offer at the easel. You might try newspaper, corrugated cardboard, or even used sandpaper scraps.

■ Keep an eye out for interesting recycled materials children can use as they create. Try adding dried leaves, seeds, and other natural items to your collection. Also include family donations and items children find.

■ Encourage unusual combinations of materials. Fabric and colored-paper scraps are not only great for collages, they also stick to wet paint.

Block Area

Listen as children build with blocks and you will hear them dealing daily with problems of construction and design as well as social problems. Comments such as, "This won't stay up!" "I need more blocks to finish my tower," and, "Your house is in my road!" are all exclamations of problem solvers at work.

■ Offer recycled materials such as juice cans, paper tubes, carpet and fabric pieces, and bits of rope in addition to unit blocks. These materials vary the types of construction problems children can solve.

■ Hang magazine photos of buildings, dams, or bridges from around the world to spark new ideas. These pictures ask — but don't answer — the problem-solving question, "How can you build something that looks like this?"

■ Leave block buildings up for more than one day so children can observe, add to, and re-create their own structures. This extra time provides new opportunities for problem solving with blocks.

Cooking Area

Preparing food — cutting, measuring, mixing, stirring — is a delicious way to put problem solving into action. Serving, eating, and cleaning up at snack- and lunchtimes present important problems,

too. By helping children solve these problems themselves, you help boost self-esteem.

■ Ask children to problem-solve and predict when following recipes. You might say, "This batter seems too dry. How can we make it wet?" "What do you think will happen when we add food coloring?"

■ Set out ingredients and invite children to invent their own recipes. Cut-up fruits and vegetables, yogurt, raisins, nuts, and granola are all excellent for individualized cooking activities.

■ Eat "family style" and involve children in setting up and cleaning after meals. When children practice pouring milk and passing plates, they learn solutions they can use for problems at home as well.

Good Books for Problem Solving

Children's storybooks can set the stage for exciting problem-solving discussions. Try reading parts of stories without revealing how the characters resolve the main problem. Then ask children what they would do. Thinking about imaginary problems in books can give children safe ways to work out problems they may be facing in real life. Here are a few story choices, along with problem-solving questions you might ask.

Cloudy With a Chance of Meatballs by Judi Barrett (Atheneum). What would you do if you were stuck in Chewandswallow? How would you get out?

Company's Coming by Arthur Yorinks (Scholastic). What would you do if space aliens landed in your backyard?

Grandfather Twilight by Barbara Berger (Philomel). Where do you think the moon comes from?

Little Fox Goes to the End of the World by Ann Tompert (Scholastic). How would you travel to the end of the world? How would you know if you arrived there?

A Special Trade by Sally Whitman (Scholastic). How would you help Grandpa? What special items would you use?

Swimmy by Leo Lionni (Pantheon). If you were Swimmy, what would you do about the big fish?

There Is a Nightmare in My Closet by Mercer Mayer (Dial Books). What could you do if you were afraid of something in your room at night?

Questions to Ask Around the Room

Use these problem-solving questions as examples to help you create more of your own:

In the Art Area:
- How many ways can you fold or rip these pieces of paper?
- What would happen if you used more than one marker at a time?
- Are there new colors you can make with the paint?
- How many different shapes can you mold your clay into?

In the Block Area:
- Can you build something that a doll can fit into? You can fit in?
- Can you build a tower as big as yourself?
- Can you construct a road as long as the room?
- How many ways can you build a bridge?

In the Cooking Area:
- What would happen if I put some salt in the water? Sugar?
- How can we pass the juice without spilling it?
- How many ways can you scramble an egg?
- How do these different bread products taste the same or different?

In the Dramatic-Play Area:
- How many ways can you use a scarf?
- What are some different ways you can carry a baby doll?
- What can you do with a cardboard box?
- What would you do to turn the dramatic-play area into a pet store?

In the Manipulatives Area:
- Which of these objects are the same or different?
- What's another way to sort these objects?
- How many different shapes can you make with these table blocks?
- Where will people sit when they ride in your car?

In the Outdoor Area:
- How many ways can you balance this beach ball between you?
- How many different ways can you move from here to there?
- Can you build a sand castle big enough to get inside?
- What would happen if the sun didn't come out?

In the Sand and Water Area:
- How can we keep sand from leaking out of this sieve?
- How many ways can you draw a line in the sand?
- Which container will hold the most water? The least?
- What can you use to make a boat that floats?

In the Science/Discovery Area:
- What would happen if you mixed these two colors together?
- How many ways can you blow bubbles?
- How far can you roll a paper tube without touching it?
- How can you make a piece of paper stick to one end of a straw?

Dramatic-Play Area

There are so many ways children problem-solve through dramatic play! Playing with props and role playing require high levels of creative thinking and social skills.

- Provide a wide variety of open-ended props. For example, scarves, clothes, and sheets in different sizes, colors, shapes, and weights can become anything from hats to aprons, blankets, and tents.

- Keep a few unusual props in a box, such as a flashlight, a giant marble, and a beach ball. Rotate the items often. This way, you say to children, "I can't wait to see how you use these!"

- Add a few props that relate to a favorite story your group is reading. See if and how children use these items to re-create the story in their play. Also ask children what they might need to act out a story or theme in the dramatic-play area.

Manipulatives Area

Children solve problems when they can build and sort with a variety of interesting materials. By considering the materials you offer, you can expand children's problem-solving opportunities.

- Provide a rotating collection of materials children can investigate, compare, and sort on trays or in cans, such as rocks, shells, and keys.

- Offer a wide range of construction materials such as small wooden blocks, foam blocks, and toys that have interlocking pieces. Allow children to try using more than one material at a time.

- Present challenges to older children. You might invite them to create something "as long as the table" or "as high as the chair." Also encourage children to invent their own challenges.

Outdoor Area

The playground is a wonderful laboratory for problem solving as children test their skills. Running, climbing, throwing, and riding all pose problems to solve.

- Observe and ask questions to help children expand problem-solving outdoors. You might ask, "Jason, how did you make the trike go backward?" "Jamie, how can you get your foot up on that bar?"

■ Provide materials for fun group problem-solving activities, such as trying to keep a balloon in the air or finding ways to move a large, heavy ball.

■ Keep activities noncompetitive. Remember, for most young children, competing can damage self-esteem.

■ Provide large, movable materials such as planks, tires, or cartons so children can create their own structures and enclosures.

Sand and Water Area

Sand and water are both natural materials for children to explore. As they ask and answer their own questions, problems of curiosity, construction, and invention happen.

■ For both sand and water, offer buckets, shovels, and different sizes of containers for children to play with every day. From time to time, add unusual materials such as tongue depressors, food coloring, and even large chunks of ice.

■ Observe the children's problem solving as they play. Be aware of the questions they seem to be investigating, such as, "How can I make this tunnel stay up?" "What can I use to make a boat?" Facilitate their efforts by asking questions and offering materials.

■ Supply child-sized brooms, dustpans, sponges, and towels. Cleaning up after themselves offers children opportunities to solve problems and build self-esteem.

Science Area

A science table is the perfect place for children to solve problems through exploration and discovery. Making predictions and testing them out are other important problem-solving activities that can happen here.

■ Rotate interesting collections of materials for children to explore independently. Ask children and parents to help you assemble these collections.

■ Group materials according to children's interests and invite them to see how the items are the same and different. If children are exploring wind, you might set out pinwheels, flags, small kites, balloons, etc.

■ Occasionally offer questions for children to investigate, such as, "What will a magnet pick up?" "How can you make a shadow?" "How far will the wind-up toy go before stopping?" Hang a chart where children can record their predictions.

■ Supply objects children can safely take apart, such as a real telephone or radio. Provide cans or other containers in which children can sort and compare the pieces.

Group-Time Area

Group time is another activity in which problems frequently arise. Often they are problems of social interaction, such as children having difficulty waiting their turn or sitting next to one another. Thinking problems also occur during group discussions. Talking together about these problems offers great opportunities for learning.

■ Involve children as much as possible in classroom routines such as acknowledging who is absent and what activities will be open.

■ Invite children to help you brainstorm solutions to group problems, such as where to place wet paintings to make sure they don't get ruined, or how to take turns talking. Accept all suggestions offered and try voting for the solution children think will work best.

■ Promote more group problem solving by asking children to help plan events. For example, you might say, "Since the weather is getting warm, I think it might be fun to have a picnic. What do you like to eat at picnics? How would we get ready?"

Creating a Problem-Solving Center

Problem-solving centers are not standard in early childhood programs. But they are perfect places for children to explore and practice critical and creative thinking.

Why do you need a special center when problem solving happens all around your room? The advantage of a problem-solving center is that it focuses on the problem-solving process. Instead of concentrating on one particular material or skill, such as science, language, or art, it brings together many curriculum areas. In fact, just calling an area a "problem-solving center" helps children become more aware of the problem solving they naturally do.

You don't need a lot of extra room or expensive materials to create a problem-solving center. Think about setting up a problem-solving center for a week or two at first. Then, later, you might decide to make it a permanent part of your room. You might want to begin by adding materials to your discovery table or science center or by expanding your art area. (See the diagram on pages 28 and 29 for a picture of what a large problem-solving center might look like.)

Stocking Your Center
Supplying the Basics

Ask children and families to help you collect a large supply of interesting scrap and recycled materials for children to investigate. Ribbons, spools, telephone wire, paper plates, plastic-foam squiggles, paper bags, and bubble paper are just a few of the possibilities. Add to or rotate the items periodically, so children always have new surprises to explore.

Include basic art materials such as paper, scissors, and tape to encourage children to build and create.

To avoid clutter and mess, organize the items in individual boxes. (Shoe boxes often work well.) Label each box with a colored shape or, for older children, a number. This way, children can find the items they want without needing to dig through a box of tangled scrap materials.

Including Problems About Science

Items that are usually found in a science or discovery area often make good materials for the problem-solving center. By placing objects to explore and take apart — sunflowers, pinecones, telephones, etc. — near art and other types of materials, you help children think of new ways to investigate. Listen for discoveries that spark children's interest, then add new materials to help them tackle these problems. For example, if children are intrigued by reflections, try adding unbreakable mirrors, aluminum foil, sunglasses, and other reflective objects. Try adding a prediction and results chart, as well, for children to write or draw about their ideas.

Including Problems About Art

Art activities can also take on new life in the problem-solving center. If your problem-solving and art centers are adjacent, you might place the easel in between to emphasize that problem solving as well as art happens there. This is also a good place to introduce materials for artistic experiments, such as adding sand, sawdust, or glitter to create textured paints.

Also, try combining art and problem solving by making "starter pictures." Draw a wiggly line on a piece of oaktag or poster board, or glue on paper cut in an interesting shape. Cover the boards with clear, self-adhesive vinyl or laminate. Children can draw on the boards with crayons or markers, then wipe them off when they are through.

Including Problems About Language

Hang unusual photos and drawings cut from books or magazines to spark interesting problem solving. For example, you might put up an advertisement showing a dog standing guard in front of a refrigerator. Ask the question, "What if this dog could talk? What do you think he would say?" Invite children to respond to this or make up a story of their own. Pictures of children who look happy, sad, or lonely can spark excellent group problem solving about feelings. You might also help remind children of safety rules by talking about pictures of children in unsafe situations, such as a child jumping from a swing or holding skates near a pond that isn't frozen.

Setting Up for Sharing

Plan a variety of ways for children to share their problem-solving solutions with others.

■ Set aside a "museum" area where they can display their creations. Supply plain white paper or five-inch by eight-inch cards that children can use to write or dictate information or stories about their creations.

■ Some children may like to draw pictures to show how they would solve problems. Pencils, markers, and crayons in this center, together with old magazines to cut, help children express their ideas through art.

■ Supply a tape recorder so children can tape their answers and stories to problem-solving questions. Then, at group time, invite children to play the tape and discuss their responses with the group. The tape recorder is an especially good way for children to record their responses to problem-solving pictures.

Problem Solving in Mixed-Age Settings

The everyday routines and mixed-age groupings of family child-care homes offer plenty of opportunities for children to find and solve problems. A relaxed, cozy setting and a patient adult can add to children's enjoyment and pride in their accomplishments.

Here are tips to keep in mind as you support and encourage children's problem solving:

■ **Involve children in daily routines.** Setting the table, putting on jackets, and cleaning up the living room are all rich opportunities for problem solving. Think about weekly and monthly routines, too. If you move pieces of equipment on Fridays and Mondays so your family has more space, consider doing some selected moving together. Work in teams and plan where and how to move each piece.

■ **Notice the problem solving infants and toddlers do on their own.** When 11-month-old Max figures out that he needs to remove his arm from inside a cupboard before he can close the door, he solves a problem — and his face beams. By letting very young children take time to solve problems, you encourage their development. At the same time, you model patience, so older children might wait a moment before stepping in to help.

■ **Encourage older children to help infants and toddlers.** Locating lost items such as boots on a crowded floor or a misplaced favorite cuddly is a great way for older children to help. Support older children's problem solving by asking questions to help them think and plan before they begin.

■ **Let the challenges of mixed-age groups become opportunities for problem solving.** For example, if an infant or toddler is threatening the block tower a four-year-old is building, invite the four-year-old to help think of appropriate solutions.

■ **Encourage cooperative problem solving.** Group time is a good time to discuss problems that affect everyone. "Cleanup time does not feel good to me. I am doing a lot of reminding. What ideas do you think will help?" Be sure everyone gets chances to offer and talk about ideas.

■ **Keep individual differences in mind.** Differences in development, plus daily considerations such as illness or feeling tired, all influence children's problem-solving abilities. Keep variations in mind and also watch for growth. Remember, a three-year-old who isn't able to put on his or her own shoes in September might be helping other children by spring!

— KATHIE SPITZLEY

Problems of the Week

Try presenting challenges in your problem-solving center on Monday and give children the entire week to work on solutions. At group time, introduce a challenge based on children's interests and show them the materials available in the problem-solving center. Together, brainstorm several possible solutions. Here are four problems, in order from easiest to most difficult, to consider presenting.

Grab Bags

Prepare grab bags filled with scrap materials, including at least one item in each that can be used as a base, such as a paper plate or tray. Show the contents of the bags at group time and ask, "What can you make with the things in these bags?" Invite children to brainstorm together. Put the bags in your center, provide glue or paste and scissors, and encourage your young inventors to create. At the end of the week, invite children to show their inventions to the group.

How Many Ways Can You ...?

These kinds of questions are excellent for the problem-solving center. Choose materials such as paper tubes, plates, or bags,

and invite children to add other scrap and art materials to create anything they like. With older children, you might suggest creating something more specific by asking, "How many ways can you use a paper tube to make something that rolls?"

Let's Make a Bird's Nest!

In this problem, the use of the object is specified instead of the materials. Invite children to use any of the materials in the problem-solving center and attempt these challenges: Can you invent something that flies? Can you build a nest for a bird? You might relate the problems to a current theme the group is focusing on. For example, if you are investigating living things, children might try to create real or imaginary three-dimensional animals.

Task-Card Fun

Older children (fours and fives) may enjoy using problem-solving task cards. Use symbols to write a problem on an index card, such as, "Use items from box 1, box 4, and box 7 to make a car." Children can "read" the problem on the card, think about how to solve it, find the materials they'll need, and start creating! Invite children to add materials from other areas of your room to complete their inventions.

These four different types of problems are models that can be used with other materials. Adapt them in your program to fit your group's interests. Remember, you are providing children with opportunities to problem-solve and, at the same time, teaching something about recycling materials in new and creative ways.

A Super Setup!

A problem-solving center with a variety of materials from different areas of your room helps stretch children's creative thinking. The illustration at left shows how such a setup can offer children unlimited possibilities. The numbers correspond to the suggestions below.

1. Display a variety of children's work that invites them to talk and write about their creations.

2. Offer lots of unusual open-ended materials, including recycled and scrap materials, so children can invent new uses for them. Neatly organize items in labeled boxes. Rotate some of the items to provide children with new challenges.

3. Hang a selection of pictures and posters to act as "story starters." Pose an open-ended question above the pictures to spark some individual and group problem-solving stories.

4. Use technology to provide more possibilities. A tape recorder offers children additional ways to record their stories and thoughts.

5. Provide a collection of laminated picture boards that children can use to draw on and problem-solve over and over again.

6. Be sure to include plenty of basic art materials such as glue sticks, scissors, construction and scrap paper, and crayons and markers. Children can use these tools to solve problems in the problem-solving center or take them elsewhere in the room.

7. Keep task cards — index cards with picture and word descriptions on them — on hand to offer challenges for older children.

8. Encourage your group to investigate problems at an open work space where they have plenty of room to explore.

LEARNING AND GROWING
With Problem Solving

Problem solving addresses the development of the whole child — socially, emotionally, physically, cognitively, and creatively. As a young child develops the ability to problem-solve, a wide range of other skills and concepts are enhanced as well.

This three-page chart identifies areas of development and important skills as they relate to problem solving. Share the chart with staff and families to enhance their understanding of the many dimensions of problem solving.

Each entry begins with a description of how a key skill relates to problem solving. "Ways to Assist" helps you enhance development. "Developmental Considerations" includes reminders of what you might expect from younger (twos and threes) and older (fours and fives) children. Since behaviors vary at all ages, use this chart as a guideline only. Be open to the individual differences you experience in your own group.

COGNITIVE DEVELOPMENT

Language Skills

Children use language skills to explore their ideas and communicate them to others. When children listen to questions and ideas and respond with their own, they are utilizing both receptive- and expressive-language skills. By listening to children's language, you get a glimpse into the ways they think and solve problems.

Ways to Assist

■ Ask open-ended questions that can't be answered with a "yes" or "no," but rather require a phrase or sentence. You might ask, "What do you think makes the leaves change color?"

■ Record children's ideas on experience charts or add them to stories so they see that their thoughts can be written down.

■ Invite children to make predictions about field trips, walks, stories in books, and natural events. You might ask, "What do you think we'll see at the firehouse?" "How will this book end?"

Developmental Considerations

■ Since younger children think in the "here and now," it's important to ask questions about their current experiences. Remember, too, that it's natural for younger children to respond with just one word.

■ Fours and fives enjoy talking about more abstract concepts than younger children and are more adept at large-group problem-solving discussions. But keep in mind that in very large groups, children sometimes simply repeat what other children have said. For more in-depth thinking, have open-ended discussions in small groups or one-on-one.

Math Skills

Problem solving is at work when children sort, measure, compare, pattern, and graph. These important math processes arise naturally through play and invite children to answer how much, how many, and how long.

Ways to Assist

■ Incorporate estimation activities into everyday events. Invite children to guess how many steps it will take to get from the door to the playground fence, or how many crackers are left in the basket. Be prepared for "wild" guesses at first, and closer approximations as children become more experienced estimators.

■ Help children make comparisons frequently by asking, "How are these the same? What is different?" Also ask, "How many ways can you sort them?" Use objects that are in your children's environment, such as the books on the shelf or children's shoes.

Developmental Considerations

■ For younger children, the numeric concept of "how many" is not as important as comparing "big and little" or "few and many." They are usually good at sorting objects by color, shape, or size, but can get confused when there are too many attributes to choose from. Use simple shapes and colors for sorting activities.

■ Older children are in transition from the concrete stage of sorting, measuring, and comparing actual objects to the more abstract stage of symbolizing their thinking using words, charts, and graphs. Help children see how their problem solving can be represented by using actual items to make graphs and measuring using pieces of yarn. You can attach the yarn pieces to poster board to make measuring charts.

Science Process Skills

When children use problem-solving skills in science experiences, they are using the steps of the scientific method — observing, predicting, experimenting, and concluding. This process often works best in the spontaneous experiments children create as they play, such as watching a hill of ants or mixing colors at the easel.

Ways to Assist

■ Model scientific problem solving by asking questions about things you observe with children, such as, "What do you think will happen if we put out some crumbs for the ants? What would happen if you mixed two colors at a time?" Accept all ideas and test them out together.

■ Provide planned problem-solving science experiences with classroom materials, such as predicting the best place to melt an ice cube or observing balls rolling down block ramps. Encourage children to talk about their experiments to help them further develop their ideas.

Developmental Considerations

■ Younger children need plenty of time to observe and experiment. They may do the same process over and over again, because they're constructing and testing out their own knowledge about how things work.

■ Older children are ready to use prediction and results charts to represent their problem-solving experiments. (See example in activity plan, page 68.) These charts help children organize their thinking and draw conclusions, because they can see direct correlations between the prediction and the results.

Learning and Growing With

CREATIVE DEVELOPMENT

Explorations With Materials

Problem-solving skills invite children to be flexible and creative thinkers and experimenters, enabling them to use materials in new and unusual ways. As they work with materials, children are creating new problems to solve and discovering that there are usually many possible ways of doing things — skills that will aid them now and throughout life.

Ways to Assist
■ Provide a setting rich with open-ended materials.

■ Encourage children to use materials in many ways, accepting their ideas as long as they are safe.

■ Ask questions that encourage children to view materials in new ways, such as, "How many ways can you use this piece of clay?"

■ Give children plenty of time to experiment. Adding a few extra minutes to your free-play time can encourage children to become much more involved.

Developmental Considerations
■ Twos and threes are naturals at creative exploration with materials. They may play in ways that might appear to be inappropriate (especially with food), but remember, creative thinking is at work. Look for ways to support their creativity while encouraging table manners, too.

■ Fours and fives like to try things in so many different ways that they sometimes use up a great deal of materials. Although we want them to feel free to explore, it's important for children to learn to recycle. For example, encourage them to save paper scraps. By doing this, you help children develop an earth-friendly attitude.

Explorations With Ideas

Children use problem-solving skills as they imagine fantasy worlds, "make pretend," and take magical trips. Wonderful open-ended phrases such as, "What would happen if ...?" and, "What can you do now ...?" come alive in children's imaginations. This type of play also stretches children's thinking since it's based on ideas and mental images instead of concrete things.

Ways to Assist
■ Invite children to take imaginary journeys with you. Pretend to take a trip to the moon or a walk in the woods. Encourage children to close their eyes and talk about what they see. You might say, "We're landing on the moon now. What should we do next?"

■ When making a transition from one activity to another, invent an imaginary field of sticky gelatin or eggshells for children to walk through.

■ Introduce pantomime. Play guessing games in which one child acts out something, such as an animal or vehicle, and the others guess what the child is pretending to be.

Developmental Considerations
■ Younger children are very concrete in their approach to imaginary play. Even though they can pretend to be something or someone, they may need to have specific props or costumes to assist them.

■ Older children delight in the abstractness of pretend play and may even have an imaginary playmate. Be open to these characters. They are an important part of many children's development.

SOCIAL/EMOTIONAL

Self-Esteem

Children's self-concept is enhanced when they see themselves as problem-solvers. Successfully handling problems gives children the feeling that they can do things themselves and have an impact on their surroundings. In a supportive environment, children learn to take safe risks and see that they are capable thinkers and doers.

Ways to Assist
■ Develop an environment where children can take risks safely.

■ Celebrate diversity! Help children be aware that you know everyone has ideas and all ideas are accepted in your setting.

■ Allow children to work at their own pace. Every child has a unique learning style and may develop faster in some areas than others.

Developmental Considerations
■ Twos and threes want to do things all by themselves, yet may not be capable of accomplishing all that they try. Find ways to support children's attempts and then, if they need assistance, involve them in the process. You might say, "Let's see if we can zip this jacket together. Do you think it will work if I hold this part and you pull?"

■ Fours and fives boldly go where younger children may not explore. Observe their ventures and support their explorations while keeping safety precautions in mind. If they need help, you might say, "I see you're working hard to count the cars going by. I wonder if there's another way you can do that so you're not so close to the fence." Instead of squelching their enthusiasm and pride, support the concept and think of an alternative together.

Problem Solving

DEVELOPMENT

Conflict Resolution

A major component of problem solving is the ability to resolve conflicts by communicating and cooperating with others. When children can express problems and find ways to work out solutions together, they learn a vital coping mechanism.

Ways to Assist

■ Help children identify the problem between them. Take time to say, "You both seem very upset. Can you each tell me what's wrong?" Encourage children to focus on the situation.

■ Ask each child to share his or her feelings. When you reassure children that they will be heard, you help take away some of the urgency they feel.

■ Invite children to suggest resolutions. If they need help, provide several options for them to consider.

■ Involve children in setting the rules for the group. If a problem keeps occurring, invite the group to brainstorm ways to solve it.

Developmental Considerations

■ Since younger children are less verbal than older children, they tend to try to resolve conflicts physically. Help them by modeling the words to express their needs and feelings.

■ Older children are not only more verbal, but can better understand that others have feelings, too. When given time to reflect during a conflict, they often calm down and listen to what the other person is saying. This developing empathy helps children to see possible resolutions.

Cooperating and Sharing

Problem-solving activities encourage children to cooperate as they investigate and experiment. Whether the problems arise from teacher-initiated activities or naturally during group play, children can learn how to work together toward a common goal.

Ways to Assist

■ Reinforce children's cooperative behavior whenever it occurs. You might say, "Isabel, thank you for helping Tommy figure out a way to share the milk." Be specific in your support so children know exactly what you're referring to.

■ Use family-style dining at snack and meals. The ability to pass around and share food is a cooperative skill that children can practice every day.

■ Plan cooperative art projects in which children share materials and work together. Younger children may want to do large floor murals and finger paintings. Older children might enjoy finding ways to construct dinosaurs out of boxes or design a bulletin board that represents the spring. Also, invite children to make "pass-along pictures" that each child can draw on.

Developmental Considerations

■ Twos and threes often prefer to play alone or beside other children, instead of with them. Encourage children to cooperate and share, but keep your expectations appropriate. Support even the smallest examples of sharing.

■ Fours and fives are more interested in cooperative play and enjoy taking turns being the "leader." Support this and also show other ways that groups can interact. For example, involve children in making democratic decisions, such as voting on what to eat for snack.

PHYSICAL DEVELOPMENT

Motor Skills

Problem solving occurs whenever children use their bodies. As they tackle new physical problems, such as climbing the stairs, drawing a picture, jumping on one foot, or figuring out how to start a zipper, they go through a process of experimentation.

Ways to Assist

■ Ask open-ended questions that invite children to problem-solve with their bodies. Questions such as, "How many ways can you move your arm?" and, "Can you do a silly walk?" encourage children to think of many possible ways to move.

■ Involve children in cooperative, non-competitive games in which they physically work together. For example, trying to keep a ball up in the air using a parachute or large sheet is both problem solving and group process in action.

■ Provide opportunities for cooperative fine-motor creations. For example, by framing a large piece of cloth netting, you can prepare a giant wall hanging that everyone can help design, decorate, and hang in your room.

Developmental Considerations

■ Younger children are always testing their bodies to see what they can do. Create a safe and supportive environment for their explorations so that they feel free to take a few risks, knowing that you are there for them.

■ Older children are becoming more proficient at large-motor activities, but some may tend to shy away from fine-motor ones. They need many opportunities to practice using these skills in open-ended ways. Art and scrap materials for free construction invite children to problem-solve using their minds and their hands.

TALKING TO FAMILIES
About Problem Solving

Problem solving may not be a topic that families of your children remember talking about in their own schooling. Many may have experienced a teacher-directed education full of memorization and skill-based lessons. Therefore, it can be difficult for families to recognize the value of problem solving in their child's education. They may want to see worksheets and craft projects coming home, because these are more familiar and represent to them what "school" is all about. A child's glorious scrap-material collage may not be valued immediately for the wonderful thinking and problem solving involved in producing it.

Many Ways to Communicate

It is important for you to help families recognize

what creative problem solving is, so they can value it as an essential part of their children's development. Here are ways to communicate to families how problem-solving experiences are not only fun, but also develop important high-level thinking skills that will serve their children throughout their

schooling and for the rest of their lives.

Hold problem-solving workshops. One of the best ways to convince parents of the value of problem solving is to help them experience it themselves. You might want to start a workshop by asking parents to do workbook pages, dittos, or coloring pages. Then ask, "What new things did you learn while doing this activity? What did you think about?"

Next, invite them to participate in problem-solving activities in different centers of the room. You could ask them to try to build a bridge with blocks using only two different shapes, or to predict which materials will absorb water, or create a vehicle using scrap materials. Then ask families to talk about which activity required the most thinking — and which was the most fun!

Copy activity plans. Many of the activity plans at the back of this book provide excellent suggestions for families to try out at home. Photocopy appropriate plans and make them available for parents to use as "recipes for a rainy day."

Send home "I did it" notes. Focus on successful problem solving in the notes you send home to families. Remark about the wonderful way a child solved a problem with a sculpture, a block structure that kept falling over, or a problem with a friend. This shows families what to look for and support in their own child's activities.

Provide open-ended questions along with books. Next time you send home books for families to borrow, add a file card with a few open-ended questions they might ask their child. By offering families frequent models, you can give them new ideas for open-ended questions to ask.

Offer articles. Articles about thinking skills and problem solving are becoming more prevalent, not only in education magazines but in popular magazines such as *Newsweek* and *Time*. Copy all or parts of easy-to-read articles to send home and underline the sections you really want parents to read!

Whatever methods you choose, remember that experience helps families understand that education is a joyful, cooperative process of children interacting with materials and people.

JAMES LEVIN

34

SHARING PROBLEM SOLVING AT HOME:
A Message to Families

Dear Family,

The ability to solve a problem — to think creatively and constructively — is an overarching skill that affects all learning. Problem solving is not memorizing facts like color and shape names or the alphabet. Instead, it is the ability to use these facts whenever and however needed. Problem solving is the "glue" that binds other skills together. As a family, what can you do to help your child develop problem-solving skills? Here are a few suggestions.

Involve Your Child: One of the most important ways you can help is to not always solve problems for children! Of course it is natural to want to help, but adults can actually disempower children by helping them too much. Your child needs to know that he or she has your support, but can still solve problems independently — or with just a little help. When you let your child help figure out how to fix a toy or solve a sibling dispute, you allow him or her to see what solutions work and also help build self-esteem.

Ask Questions: Consider the ways you talk with your child. Do you ask many questions or usually offer answers or give information? Try asking open-ended questions that have many possible answers. These questions help children feel safe to take "risks" without fear of being wrong. "What would happen if …?" "Did you ever wonder …?" "How many ways can you …?" are all great open-ended question starters. Often, the questions children ask you are the best ones to ask them! When your child asks, "Why is the sky blue?" or, "Where do rainbows come from?" you can say, "What do you think?" Be prepared for some wonderfully creative ideas.

Share Stories: When you read a book together, stop at a crucial point and ask your child to pretend to solve the character's problem. You might ask, "What would you do if you were in the story?" Or

try a crazy question like, "What would happen if the giant in *Jack in the Beanstalk* were an alligator? How would the story be different?" "How would you change the ending of *The Three Little Pigs*?" Open-ended questions such as these can add a wonderful new flavor to your bedtime reading and encourage problem solving at the same time.

Take It Slowly: Problem solving is an art, and it takes time. It might often seem easier and faster for you to jump in and show your child how to button a jacket or fit a piece in a puzzle. But try to be patient! Stop, take a deep breath, and allow him or her the precious time needed to conquer the problem. The independence your child learns will ultimately save you both time. And the experience will help develop a happy child with strong self-esteem, because he or she can say, "I did it myself!"

Happy Problem Solving!
Sincerely,

_____

Teacher

Using the Activity Plans

The following 40 pages offer suggestions for developmentally appropriate activities to help enhance children's problem solving. The activity plans provide ideas for helping children solve problems in a variety of curriculum areas, including science, math, art, and language, as well as problems that arise through social interaction. Use these activities to complement and extend children's own problem solving to create a rich, stimulating learning environment.

Getting the Most From the Activity Plans

Because each plan is designed with a specific age in mind, the set together offers help in planning problem-solving experiences that are developmentally appropriate to the interests and abilities of twos, threes, fours, and fives. Of course, these ages represent a wide range of developmental levels, so you may find that you need to adapt certain plans for your particular group. To truly get the most from the plans, look at all 40 for ideas to simplify, modify, or extend.

The format is simple and easy to follow. Each plan includes most of these sections:

■ **Aim** — the value of the activity is explained through a list of the skills and concepts that the plan develops more fully.

■ **Group Size** — the suggested number of children to involve at one time. Adjust this to your own needs.

■ **Materials** — basic materials and special items to gather are suggested here.

■ **In Advance** — materials to prepare or arrangements to make before introducing an activity.

■ **Getting Ready** — ways to introduce the activity theme to one child, a small group, or a large group of children. Open-ended questions

help children think and talk about topics related to the activity.

■ **Begin** — suggestions for introducing materials, helping children get started, and guiding the activity in nondirective ways. Some of the plans also offer suggestions for ways to bring the activity to a close, as well as extension ideas to further enhance an experience.

■ **Remember** — developmental considerations to keep in mind, an occasional safety reminder, and tips about ways to relate other skills and concepts to the activity theme.

■ **Books** — carefully selected children's books that relate to the activity plan's topic, or professional books where you can look for additional ideas.

Colleagues, aides, volunteers, and family members can all benefit from suggestions for child-centered problem-solving activities. So feel free to duplicate and share each plan for educational use. Remember, when you share activity plans, you offer not only ideas, but a philosophy of learning and creativity as well.

Using the Activity Index

The index on pages 78-79 lists each activity plan, along with the developmental areas and skills it enhances. Use the index to:

■ Determine the full range of skills and concepts covered in the plans.

■ Highlight specific skills or developmental areas a plan reinforces when talking with family members.

■ Identify and locate an activity that reinforces a particular skill on which you want to focus.

■ Assist in finding activities that complement your group's current interests.

ACTIVITY PLANS

For Twos, Threes, Fours, and Fives

? | PROBLEM SOLVING

How is sand different when you add water? Invite twos to find out.

DRY TO WET

Aim: Children will practice thinking and language skills as they play with dry and wet sand.

Group Size: Two to four children.

Materials: A sandbox, sand table, or several basins filled about halfway with sand; several small plastic buckets or other containers; sand toys such as strainers or sieves; and a water source.

GETTING READY

Throughout your day, encourage children to identify things that are wet and things that are dry. For example, touch the soil before watering plants. Ask, "Is this soil dry? Is it wet?" Then add water together and talk about the changes. Look for other opportunities, such as when children wash and dry their hands or help sponge tables.

BEGIN

Gather outdoors in a clean sandbox or near your sand table or basins filled with sand. Observe for a while as children play freely with the sand. Talk about how it feels. Ask if it feels wet or dry. After children have had plenty of time to play, put out a few containers filled with water. As you do, ask twos what they think will happen if you pour water in the sand.

Then let them try it out. As they pour, talk about what's happening. Feel the sand together and talk about it using descriptive words such as *wet, dark,* and *cool.* Allow children to add as much water as they'd like, and continue talking about the changes they see and feel. You might say, "Lee added a little water. It made the sand feel a little bit wet. Vivien poured lots of water near her. How is her sand changing?" As children play, comment on their actions and point out other ways the wet and dry sand are the same and different. You might say, "Larry, you are sifting the dry sand through the strainer. But the wet sand doesn't sift through Jackie's strainer. It stays inside."

Remember

■ Be prepared for sand and water to overflow onto the floor and onto children. Wear smocks and use a floor covering such as a large towel or drop cloth.

■ Outdoor sand play is a good opportunity to watch children's experimentations and social interactions.

Do they try things outdoors that are different from indoors? Do they prefer to play alone or with others? Make notes of your observations to help you document children's development.

BOOKS

These resource books include science and problem-solving activities for very young children.

• *Bubbles, Rainbows, and Worms* by Sam Ed Brown (Gryphon House)

• *Rub-a-Dub-Dub, Science in the Tub* by James Lewis (Meadowbrook Press)

• *Small Wonders: Hands-on Science Activities for Young Children* by Peggy K. Perdue (Scott, Foresman & Co.)

PROBLEM SOLVING

Hands are the tools to use when solving these simple problems of categorization.

WHAT IS SOFT? WHAT IS HARD?

Aim: Children will use problem solving and the sense of touch to decide if items are soft or hard.

Group Size: Three or four children.

Materials: Items from around your room that feel hard (at least one for each child), such as blocks, markers, plastic bowls, or puzzle pieces; and items that feel soft (also at least one for each child), such as stuffed animals, towels, clothes from your dramatic-play area, and foam blocks.

GETTING READY

Gather in a cozy spot and talk about hands. Invite children to tell you things they know about hands. What can they do? How do they help us? Together, have fun wiggling your fingers and showing how hands can hold and grasp. Use your hands to touch a few things around you and talk about how they feel.

BEGIN

Bring the soft items to a cozy area and gather with twos. Let each child choose one soft item to hold, and keep one for yourself. Join in as everyone uses hands to feel his or her item. You might say, "This shirt feels soft. It feels nice in my hands and against my cheek." Rub the item gently against your face and encourage twos to try the same motion using their items. Talk about what they feel. Then ask, "What else feels soft in your hands? This rug feels soft in mine." Together, look around the room for other items and decide if they feel soft. As twos point out items, ask, "Does it feel soft in your hands? Does it feel nice against your cheek?"

Another time, bring the hard items to a spot on a rug and gather again. Let each child choose one hard item and repeat the process, this time talking about "hard." Try tapping your hard item against your hand, and talk about what happens. You might say, "This block feels hard. When I tap it, it makes a noise." Invite children to try tapping their items, and talk about the results. Now, look around the room for more hard items. Encourage children to feel and tap, using their hands, to decide if items are hard. Continue talking about hard and soft as children touch different items throughout the day.

Remember

■ Twos might want to talk about other features of their items, such as color or texture. Accept these responses and help build vocabulary by using appropriate words, such as *smooth, bumpy,* and *scratchy.*

■ Many children might be more intrigued by using hard items to make sounds than by talking about "hard." Allow them to follow their interests and extend the activity in new directions.

BOOKS

These are books about hands and touching.

- *I Touch*
  by Helen Oxenbury
  (Walker)

- *My Hands Can*
  by Jean Holzenthaler
  (E.P. Dutton)

- *Sticky Stanley*
  by Thomas Crawford
  (Troll)

? PROBLEM SOLVING

Cleanup is problem solving for twos!

WHERE DOES IT GO?

Aim: Twos will practice classification, matching, and self-help skills by helping to put away toys.

Group Size: Your whole group.

Materials: Toys and toy shelves already in your program, construction paper, clear adhesive paper, markers, and scissors (for adult use).

In Advance: Consider the toys available at free play and mentally group them into categories — vehicles, blocks, dolls, dress-up items, dishes and cooking items, etc. Also note the storage areas where each group of toys is stored.

On construction paper, draw a picture or silhouette of a few items representing each group. For example, you might draw a hat and a shoe to represent dress-up items, a pot and a spoon to represent kitchen items, or a car and truck to represent vehicles. Cut out the pictures or silhouettes. Then, using clear adhesive paper, attach them to the bins, shelves, trunks, drawers, and cabinets where those items are stored.

BEGIN

If you don't already have a cleanup-time routine, make one a regular part of your day. The end of free play, the transition before lunch or nap, or the end of the day are all good for cleaning up. During these times, invite everyone to help pick up the toys and materials that were played with. As each child picks up an item, ask, "Where does it go?" Help children understand that the pictures you placed around the room can help them figure out where things belong. For example, you might say, "Tony, the blocks go in this bin that has the picture of blocks on the outside." When an item isn't pictured exactly, such as a scarf that's part of the dress-up area, talk about where it might go. You might say, "A scarf can go on your head like a hat. Should we put it in the drawer that has a picture of a hat?" Help children in this way the first few times you introduce your cleanup routine. After a while, children will get into the habit of putting toys away.

Remember

■ Twos often enjoy helping. Be sure to treat cleaning as a fun activity rather than a chore.

■ Some children might not want to help clean up. Positively acknowledge those who do help. Eventually, most children will join in.

■ Make storage labels even for items that are accessible only to teachers but safe for children to touch, such as paint bottles and play dough. Then twos can go to the appropriate storage area and point to or ask for the items when they want to use them.

BOOKS

Here are a few cleanup-time books.

• *Time to Clean*
by Valerie J. Meler
(Modern Publishing)

• *Where Can It Be?*
by Ann Jonas
(Greenwillow Books)

• *Where's My Truck?*
by Anne Sibley O'Brien
(Henry Holt)

PROBLEM SOLVING

Pretending to care for babies offers lots of problems for twos to solve.

WHAT CAN WE DO?

Aim: Twos will use the math skills of one-to-one correspondence and reasoning to solve everyday problems.
Group Size: Four children at a time.
Materials: A well-stocked dramatic-play area, with enough dolls, blankets, bowls, spoons, etc., for you and each child to have one of each.

BEGIN

In your housekeeping or dramatic-play area, set out bowls, spoons, blankets, and other items. Invite children to join you. Give a doll to each child and ask, "What do we need to take care of baby?" If children hesitate, you can be more specific and say, "My baby needs to eat some food. What could I use to feed her?" Encourage children to look for things to eat with. Point to the items you set out and ask, "Do you think we could use these?"

As children begin to collect items for their babies, point out that each one has a bowl, a spoon, and a blanket. Some children may want all the blankets, or to take all the spoons. Help children learn to recognize and solve these conflicts. You might say, "Justin has two spoons for his baby and Trisha doesn't have any for her baby. What can we do?" Encourage children to think about the problem and express their ideas for solving it.

Next — whether or not children solve the conflict — redirect them by posing another situation. "Baby is sleepy. What can we do? What do we need to put the baby to sleep?" Encourage verbalization by holding up a blanket or pillow and asking, "What's this? Can we use this to give baby a nap?" As children begin playing, step back and observe as they handle situations that occur. If necessary, intervene to ask, "What can we do?"

Remember

■ As they play, some twos may emerge as verbal and commanding, while other children may stay quiet and follow others' lead. Still others may engage in parallel play, alone yet near the group. All these styles are normal for developing twos.

■ Learning to recognize and solve conflicts is an important step toward developing self-control. To assist your twos, you can:
• Be sure enough items are available so every child can feel ownership. Twos must learn this concept before they can understand sharing.
• Have a toy or other object ready to give to a child who may end up without a disputed item.
• Help children express their feelings of anger and disappointment.
• Keep in mind that twos' concept of fairness is different from adults' — a child holding a doll may feel equal to a child with two blankets and three bowls.

BOOKS

Share these children's books about feelings.

• *MINE!*
by Linda Hayward
(Random House)

• *I Didn't Want to Be Nice*
by Jones Orlando
(Bradbury Press)

• *I Was So Mad*
by Mercer Mayer
(Western)

? PROBLEM SOLVING

Creativity flows as children make choices and experiment.

AN OPEN ART BAR

Aim: Twos practice decision-making skills as they choose materials and methods to use in art projects.

Group Size: Four to six children at a time.

Materials: A cabinet or cart with at least two shelves at twos' eye level; several small baskets and cans; a basin or bucket; paper such as construction paper, newsprint, wax paper, cardboard, and wrapping paper; art tools such as paintbrushes, glue, tape, and craft sticks; painting and drawing materials such as tempera paint, markers, crayons, and chalk; and collage materials such as cotton balls, sequins, leaves, cloth, and tissue-paper pieces.

In Advance: To set up your art bar, place the various types of paper on a shelf in your cabinet or cart. Place the tools in a different area, the painting and drawing materials in another area, and the collage materials in a fourth area. Use containers such as baskets and cans as needed. Using construction paper, make silhouettes to mark where each material belongs. Set the basin or bucket on your art table.

BEGIN

Point out the new art bar. As children come over to investigate, show them all the materials that are available and explain in simple terms how they are organized. Then ask,

"Would you like to make something with these materials? What would you like to use?" Give children time to think and decide what they want. You might need to help them choose. Once they've chosen the materials, step back and observe as twos create. They might use the same materials over and over, try new ones, or combine materials in new ways. Leave plenty of time and encourage children to experiment freely. As they finish using materials, remind them to put the items back on the art bar. Ask them to place paintbrushes in the basin or bucket for washing. Over time, continue to encourage children to use the art bar. Help each child by offering choices until he or she becomes comfortable with the routine.

Remember

■ Providing many unfamiliar materials at once can overwhelm twos. Introduce the art bar only when children have had experience with drawing, painting, and gluing.

■ Choosing from several options is an important part of problem solving. Offer twos as many chances as possible to choose.

■ Make art-bar-type activities the rule, not the exception, at your art table. They offer richer experiences than more teacher-directed projects.

BOOKS

These books about making choices and art are appropriate for twos.

• *Doing* (Brimax Books)

• *My First Look at Colors, a Dorling Kindersly Book* (Random House)

• *What Can You Do?* by Angela Littler (Simon & Schuster)

PROBLEM SOLVING

Gluing and stacking make creative art projects for twos.

BUILDING SCULPTURES

Aim: Twos will use gross-motor and fine-motor skills to create three-dimensional art.

Group Size: Two or three children.

Materials: Shoe boxes (one for each child); newspaper; masking tape; glue; found objects or scraps such as large empty thread spools, large buttons, pebbles, yarn or ribbon pieces, small jar lids, pompons, straws, cardboard cut into any-shaped hand-sized pieces, 35mm film cases, cardboard paper-towel tubes cut into two- to four-inch-long rings, kitchen sponges halved or quartered, pipe cleaners, cotton balls, jewelry-sized boxes and lids, and tongue depressors or ice cream sticks; an unbreakable plate for glue; smocks; and wet paper towels.

In Advance: Fill shoe boxes with crumpled newspaper and tape the lids on securely. Cover a worktable with newspaper and tape it down. Place the "found" objects in the center of the table. Pour glue into the plate until the bottom is covered and place it in the center of the table. Keep the glue bottle handy for quick refills.

BEGIN

Invite a few children to come to the art table. Explain that you will be using glue and need to wear smocks to keep it off your clothes. After you've helped children put on their smocks, let each choose a shoe box. Tell them that, using the things on the table, they can build a sculpture. You might say, "Our sculptures will be made by putting lots of things together to make one." Ask each child to pick something that he or she would like to glue onto her box. As one child holds an object, show her how to dab it into the glue and attach it to the box. Encourage children to use more pieces if they wish. As they add objects, describe what they are doing and the problems they are solving. "Rebecca, I see you're taking a pompon for your sculpture. Where will you put it?" "Manuel, you're using the cardboard tube. How can you glue it to your box?" When each child finishes, write her name wherever she chooses on her sculpture and place it on newspaper on a cabinet top or high shelf. Allow to dry for 24 hours. Remember to give each child a wet paper towel to wipe the glue off her hands.

Remember

■ Keep objects children will use for their sculptures the size of their hands or larger. If pieces are smaller, children may choke on them.

■ Some twos will spend their time seeing how many ways one object can be placed on their boxes. Remember, discovery and experimentation are more important than the number of pieces used.

■ Some twos will try to put everything on their boxes. Make sure you've collected plenty of materials so there will be enough for everyone.

■ Some twos may get upset if glue gets on their hands. Help them hold objects between their fingers, dip into the glue, and place them on their boxes to minimize the amount of glue on their hands. Keep wet paper towels handy.

■ Exploration, problem solving, and creativity are the goals. The sculpture is merely the result.

BOOKS

Share these books about building.

• *The Secret Birthday Message* by Eric Carle (Thomas Y. Crowell)

• *I Can Build a House* by Shigeo Watanabe (Philomel Books)

• *The Surprise* by George Shannon (Greenwillow Books)

? _____ PROBLEM SOLVING

Look at this picture. What do you see? Take a few minutes to discuss it with me!

PICTURE TALK

Aim: Children will use language and cognitive skills to talk about what they see in pictures.

Group Size: Four to six children at a time.

Materials: Pictures, photos, books, magazines, scissors, glue, construction paper, and clear adhesive paper.

In Advance: Look in magazines and books for pictures to cut out. The pictures should be large (at least three by five inches) and clear, showing a few objects or actions that are familiar to twos. Glue the pictures onto construction paper, cover with clear adhesive paper, and hang at children's eye level. You might want to choose pictures that represent the same theme, such as families, animals, feelings, or food.

BEGIN

When you notice a child or children looking at the pictures, join them for a discussion. Ask them to talk about what they see in the picture. Accept and affirm all interpretations. Then ask more questions to encourage more talking, always leaving plenty of time for twos to observe and respond. For example, if you're looking at a picture of a mother using a spoon to feed a baby, you might start by pointing to the spoon and asking, "What do you see here?" Or, ask, "Can you see the baby's mouth? Where is your mouth?" (When you encourage children to relate what they see to their own experiences, you help them make sense of what they see.)

Also ask questions about what's happening in the picture. "What do you think the baby is doing?" "How do you think he's feeling? Do you think he's hungry?" Be sure your questions follow and build on children's comments. Continue talking as long as children remain interested. When you're finished, leave the pictures out for more independent viewing. You might notice twos talking about the pictures by themselves or with one another.

Remember

■ Be sure the pictures you include are nonsexist and multicultural. Invite families to help you find them by looking through magazines they have at home.

■ Ask open-ended questions and keep your tone conversational. Make sure twos know that they're involved in a discussion, not a drill!

■ It's usually best to start by identifying familiar objects in the pictures, because these questions are easiest for most twos to answer. Questions that ask what's happening and what people might be feeling require twos to interpret the pictures, a more difficult cognitive skill.

■ Some twos will observe but not participate verbally. Pointing to objects while nodding may be their only responses. Help by providing words, while at the same time accepting and encouraging all forms of participation.

BOOKS

Add these to your bookshelves.

• *A Day in the Park* by Jeffrey Dinardo (Modern Publishing)

• *What Can You Do?* by Maureen Galvani (Simon & Schuster)

• *Let's Do It Together* by Amy MacDonald (Candlewick Press)

PROBLEM SOLVING

Yes, it's fun to say "no"!

NO!

Aim: Twos will use problem-solving skills and have opportunities say "no" in appropriate situations.

Group Size: Four to six children at a time.

Materials: A few props from around your room or your dramatic-play area, such as a hat, a shoe, a doll, a plastic bowl, and a teddy bear; and a large cardboard box.

BEGIN

Place all the items in the cardboard box. Invite several children to come sit with you in a cozy spot and see what's inside. Pull out an item and identify it together. Then ask a question about it that's a little bit silly. For example, if you pull out a hat, you might place it on your knee and ask, "Does this hat go on my knee?" Twos might or might not respond to your question. Move the hat to your head and emphatically say, "No! The hat goes on my head!" Let children see that it's okay to be a little silly and say a loud "noooooo" in this activity. Then repeat the question, using a different place for the hat to go. You might put the hat on a child's foot and ask,

"Does the hat go on your foot? No! The hat goes on your ..." Wait a moment to give children a chance to say "head." (You might need to say it for them.) Then place the hat on a child's head. Pull out another object and again ask another question for which the answer is "no." Continue having fun asking questions and saying "No!" about the remaining objects. Give children a chance to ask questions, too.

You might continue the activity by asking silly questions throughout the day. For example, you might ask, "Is this Mandy?" "No, this is Andrew!" "Is this Becky's daddy?" "No! This is Brian's daddy!"

Remember

■ Twos need to have a sense of control over their lives. You can help them feel in control (and avoid many power struggles) by offering opportunities to say "no" appropriately and, more importantly, by respecting their wishes not to do things. Twos who are empowered with real feelings of control tend to be much more giving, gentle, sympathetic, and tolerant of others.

BOOKS

Try these books for some fun reading.

- *How Do I Put It On?* by Shigeo Watanabe (Philomel Books)

- *A Frog Doesn't Gallop* by Joe Messerli (Modern Publishing)

- *Do I Have to Go Home?* by Karen Erickson (Viking Penguin)

PROBLEM SOLVING

**When conflicts arise,
twos can help find solutions.**

HOW CAN WE SHARE IT?

Aim: Children will learn about sharing and use problem-solving skills to determine what to do when two children want the same thing at the same time.
Group Size: Two or more children.
Materials: Toys and equipment from around your room.

BEGIN

Look for times when conflicts arise because two children want to use the same toy. Then help children follow the problem-solving process to find solutions. Begin by helping them identify the problem. For example, you might say, "Darnell is riding the trike. Annie, you want to ride it, too, don't you?

What can we do? How can we share it?" Remind children of the rule in your program that fits the situation, such as, "When one child is playing with a toy, another child can't take it away." Then give them time to think and offer a solution. Talk about their ideas and decide together if they will solve the problem. If children don't offer a solution, suggest one yourself. You might say, "Cooperating is a way to share. Maybe Annie can push Darnell on the trike. Then, in a little while, you can trade places. Darnell can push Annie."

Other solutions are possible, too. One alternative is taking turns. Suggest that Annie do another activity while she waits for Darnell to finish riding. Then she can take her turn. Pretend play is another alternative. Invite Darnell to be a truck driver or a motorcycle rider and Annie to be a traffic officer who tells Darnell when to stop and when to go. Other children might also like to join in the play, for example, as mommies or daddies who need to cross the street. Get involved by showing children how the traffic officer can stop the truck so the people can cross. After a few minutes, suggest that children change roles. Look for other conflict situations in which you can help twos problem-solve ways to share.

Remember

■ Build decision making into the process as much as possible. Allow children to choose which solution they'll use and how to implement it. In this example, Annie might choose which activity she wants to do while she waits, or what role to take in pretend play.
■ Take care not to offer too many solutions to choose from. More than two or three is confusing to most twos.
■ Sharing is something two-year-olds are just beginning to learn. By constantly reinforcing rules and demonstrating sharing techniques, you help twos understand and practice sharing.
■ The best and easiest way to handle twos in groups is to have more than one of every toy. But when this isn't possible, remember, the conflicts that arise provide opportunities for twos to practice important social skills.

BOOKS

Here are good books about sharing.

• *Mine!*
by Linda Hayward
(Random House)

• *Be My Friend*
by Anna Ross
(Random House)

• *Waiting My Turn*
by Karen Erickson
(Viking Penguin)

PROBLEM SOLVING

Here's a fun matching game for twos as they play dress-up.

SHOE MATCHING

Aim: Twos will use one-to-one correspondence and matching to solve problems as they play dress-up and try on shoes.

Group Size: Four to six children.

Materials: Shoes of several styles; dress-up accessories including hats of several styles, scarves, sunglasses, gloves, jackets, purses, beaded necklaces, and neckties; and usual dramatic-play props such as dolls and beds for dolls, kitchen utensils, chairs, tables, bowls, pots and pans, and other household items.

In Advance: If possible, purchase several styles of inexpensive shoes (slippers, dress shoes for both men and women, flip-flops or beach sandals, boots, and athletic shoes). If you aren't able to purchase new shoes, make sure old ones are sanitized by washing and disinfecting as follows: Machine-wash slippers and canvas shoes. Spray leather shoes with a bleach solution and wipe dry with paper towels. (To make bleach solution, use one part bleach to ten parts water. Put it in a clearly labeled spray bottle. Keep out of twos' reach.) Vinyl shoes can be machine-washed and air-dried.

BEGIN

Invite several children to the dramatic-play area and sit around the pile of shoes. Ask children to take off their shoes (by themselves, if possible) but keep on their socks. Hand each child a different shoe. Ask children if they can find the shoe that matches it. If a child picks a shoe that is not a match, put the two shoes side by side and talk about whether they are the same or different. Use lots of language to describe the shoes and label each kind. For example, you might say, "This shoe is a man's shoe. This shoe is a slipper. The man's shoe is brown and the slipper is blue. Can you find a brown shoe that is the same as this one?" As a child finds a match, point to the accessories and ask, "What can you find to wear with these shoes?" Allow children plenty of time to pick and wear whatever they please, and refrain from controlling their natural play. Some twos may make matches that seem illogical to you. Keep in mind that they need to make choices for themselves and that their matches may be

very logical to them. Stand back and allow children to play at their own pace and in their own ways.

Leave the shoes and dress-up clothes out so children can use them during free-play time.

Remember

■ Do not be concerned about shoes being on the correct feet. That skill will be learned much later. Children this age may not be ready to make this distinction yet.

■ For easy matching, find or purchase pairs of shoes that are as different as possible in description and style. Check out discounted department or shoe stores, which often have interesting shoes on sale.

■ Hats need to be clean, too. Make sure you use plastic ones, or experiment with washing them in machines. Often the results are more fun than the originals.

BOOKS

Share these fun books about shoes.

- *Whose Shoe?* by Margaret Miller (Greenwillow Books)

- *Boot Weather* by Judith Vigna (Albert Whitman)

- *Pajamas* by Livingston and Maggie Taylor (Gulliver Books)

? PROBLEM SOLVING

Turn your water table into a seaway with this creative challenge.

MAKE A BOAT TO FLOAT

Aim: Children will use creative-thinking, problem-solving, and fine-motor skills to design and build a boat that floats.

Group Size: Four to six children.

Materials: A variety of items to use to make boats, such as large and small wood pieces, craft sticks, large and small plastic-foam pieces and trays, plastic containers, lids, egg cartons, milk or juice containers, aluminum foil, cardboard, construction paper, and toothpicks; clear masking tape; paper clips; and several pairs of scissors.

In Advance: Ask family members to help you collect boat-making materials. On the day of the activity, set the materials on a work space near your water table. Display pictures of different kinds of boats.

BEGIN

Show children the materials. Talk together about how they might use these items to make boats that float. Accept all their responses and encourage them to talk to one another about their ideas. Now invite each child to make a boat, then place it in the water table to see if it sinks or floats.

Step back and observe as children work with the materials. You'll probably notice that some children choose a single material to place in the water, while others make elaborate constructions. As they test the boats, ask them to comment on what happens. Does their boat sink? Does it float? If it sinks, ask open-ended questions to help children think about and solve the problem. You might ask, "Why do you think it sank? What could you do to make it float?" If children want further help, you might ask, "Could you add something to your boat? Could you take something away?" Encourage children to try different solutions or make a new boat, if they prefer. Invite children to play with their boats as long as they remain interested.

Load Them Up!

Another time, offer small objects for children to place on toy boats, such as marbles, small wooden figures, or manipulatives. Experiment and talk about what happens when boats carry "cargo."

Remember

■ This activity works best after children have had plenty of opportunity to explore sinking and floating through water play.

■ Some children may be reluctant to put their boats in the water. This is fine. They may change their minds when they see other children testing their boats.

BOOKS

These are books on a floating theme.

• *Who Sank the Boat?* by Pamela Allen (Putnam Publishing Group)

• *Sheep on a Ship* by Nancy Shaw (Houghton Mifflin)

• *Mr. Gumpy's Outing* by John Burningham (Henry Holt)

? | PROBLEM SOLVING

To solve this problem, just use your ears!

WHAT MAKES THAT SOUND?

Aim: Children will use identification, matching, and other problem-solving skills as they explore sounds.

Group Size: Two to four children.

Materials: Eight small- to medium-sized opaque plastic containers with tight-fitting lids, such as yogurt or spreadable cheese containers or 35mm film cases; a variety of small noisemaking items such as sand, pebbles, marbles, metal hardware, small bells, toothpicks, beads, and coins; clear, heavy tape; a long strip of construction paper (about 3 by 18 inches); and a marker.

In Advance: Create eight sound shakers by putting one type of noisemaking item into each container. Cover, and seal with tape. On the strip of heavy paper, glue a sample of each item, and label. Keep the strip out of sight until later. Ask children if they would like to help.

BEGIN

Put the sound shakers on your science or discovery table. Encourage children to play with the shakers and listen to the sounds they make. As they explore, ask them what might be making the sounds they hear. Accept all responses. After some discussion, bring out the paper strip you prepared. Explain that the items on the strip are the same kinds you used to make the shakers. Then invite children to try to figure out which item makes the sound they hear in each one. Encourage them to shake the containers, examine the samples on the strip, and talk to one another about their ideas. Continue until children finish exploring the possibilities and seem satisfied that they've figured out what's in each. Then open them carefully and talk about what you see inside. Reseal the shakers carefully and set them on your discovery table for independent exploration.

Remember

■ Some children may want to open the shakers right away. Encourage them to use their ears, not their eyes, to figure out what's inside.

■ As an extension, you might make pairs of identical sound shakers. Encourage children to match the shakers using only sounds.

BOOKS

Here are a few books about sounds.

- *City Sounds* by Rebecca Emberley (Little, Brown)

- *Polar Bear, Polar Bear, What Do You Hear?* by Bill Martin, Jr. (Henry Holt)

- *Wheel Away!* by Dayle Ann Dodds (HarperCollins)

? PROBLEM SOLVING

Invite threes to discover the magic of colors.

COLOR MIXING

Aim: Children will experiment with making new colors by mixing red, yellow, and blue.

Group Size: Four children.

Materials: Six plastic eyedroppers; six baby-food jars, plastic ice-cube trays, or other small, clear containers; red, yellow, and blue food coloring; coffee filters, paper towels, or other absorbent white paper (a few pieces for each child); and newspaper.

In Advance: Cover your art table with newspaper or other protective material. Pour water into the baby-food jars or ice-cube trays until they're about half full, then add about five drops of food coloring to each jar. Make two jars of red water, two of yellow, and two of blue. Place the eyedroppers in the jars and put the jars on the table. Place the filters or absorbent paper nearby (but not on the table, in case of spills).

BEGIN

Gather at your art table. Show children the filters and demonstrate how to use an eyedropper to pick up the colored water. Talk about the colors children see and what colors they'd like to make on their papers. Accept all responses. Then offer a filter to each child. Help with the eyedroppers as needed as children begin to drop colored water on their filters. Talk about colors while they work, and ask questions to help children notice how the colors mix. For example, you might ask, "What happens when two colors meet? How many different colors do you think you can make?" As they notice new colors appearing on their filters, you might ask, "How did you get that color?" When filters become very wet, ask children to set them out on newspaper or hang them on a clothesline to dry. Then offer fresh filters and invite them to continue experimenting.

Later, display the filters to promote more discussion about color. (Colored filters look especially bright and pretty hanging in a window, though the sunlight will eventually cause them to fade.) Also, set out red, yellow, and blue paint at your easels to offer another way for children to experiment with color mixing.

Remember

■ Encourage discussion about colors as children experiment. However, don't insist that they name colors correctly or identify each one.

■ Some children may be more interested in experimenting with the eyedropper than in mixing colors. Suggest, but don't require, that they try mixing.

■ During the activity, the newspaper protecting the art table will likely become quite colorful. Watch to see if children notice and talk about this phenomenon among themselves.

■ Threes will likely get some of the color on their hands but should avoid getting it in their hair or eyes or on their clothes. Diluted food coloring washes out fairly well, though it often requires several washings. Be sure children wear smocks. If color gets in children's eyes, rinse immediately with cool water.

BOOKS

Add these books about colors to your shelves.

- *Mouse Paint* by Ellen Stohl Walsh (Harcourt Brace Jovanovich)
- *Who Said Red?* by Mary Serfozo (Macmillan)
- *Freight Train* by Donald Crews (Greenwillow Books and Scholastic)

? PROBLEM SOLVING

For these collages, children can fold, bend, or tear — but no cutting!

IT'S NO-SCISSORS DAY!

Aim: Children use creative-thinking and reasoning skills to explore ways to change the size and shape of paper.

Group Size: Four to six children.

Materials: Large pieces of colorful paper, such as construction paper, tissue paper, and wrapping paper; a variety of interesting magazines and catalogs; glue or tape; and a few sheets of construction paper (about 9 by 12 inches) for each child.

In Advance: Put all scissors away in cabinets or another location where children won't see them. Then set up your art table for a collage activity.

BEGIN

Gather with a small group at your art table and let each child choose a sheet of construction paper. Show children the materials and explain that today you're going to make collages without using scissors. Together, talk about how children might remove pictures from catalogs and change the sizes and shapes of the colorful paper for their collages. Accept all their responses. Then encourage children to choose materials and try out their ideas. Step back and observe as they work. You

may see children tear the paper, fold it into flat or three-dimensional shapes, or crumple it into balls. Some children might simply glue the large pieces onto their sheets of construction paper. Comment positively on what you see children doing. For example, you might say, "Nadine, I see you're folding the paper to make it smaller. You made some great shapes!" When children are finished, help them set their work out to dry. Then display it in your room at children's eye level. Encourage them to talk about their creations.

Remember

■ Offer this activity only after children have had other opportunities to make collages.

■ Some children may have trouble getting started. Help them by asking open-ended questions such as, "What do you want to glue on your paper? How big a piece do you want? How can you make it that size?" If children still have difficulty, suggest that they watch other children or ask them for help.

■ Consider holding additional no-scissors days to continue this artistic challenge. Or, vary the activity by removing the tape, glue, or staplers for a day.

BOOKS

Inspire new ideas with these books that feature collage illustrations.

• *One, Two, Three* by Brian Wildsmith (Oxford University Press)

• *Brown Bear, Brown Bear, What Do You See?* by Bill Martin, Jr. (Henry Holt)

• *Red Leaf, Yellow Leaf* by Lois Ehlert (Harcourt Brace Jovanovich)

? PROBLEM SOLVING

Have fun solving these real-life picture riddles.

"WHO IS WHO?"

Aim: Children will use language and reasoning skills and their developing sense of self and others to match baby pictures with children in their group.

Group Size: Two to four children at a time.

Materials: A baby picture of each child in the room (three by five inches or smaller), index cards (three by five inches), a pen or pencil, a small unbreakable mirror, plastic pocket-pages used in photo albums, yarn or a stapler, and a photo album (optional).

In Advance: Ask each family to send in a small baby picture of their child. Explain how the pictures will be used.

GETTING READY

On the day a child brings in his or her picture, take a few minutes to talk one-to-one. Listen as she describes her baby picture. Then ask, "How are you different now from when you were a baby? Can you tell me something about yourself that I can write down?" Record the child's responses on an index card. You might ask additional questions to help her get started, such as, "What can you do now? What do you look like?" Provide a mirror so she can study her image. When the child finishes, invite her to help you put the baby picture in one pocket-page and the index card in the pocket next to it. Repeat this process with each child until everyone has a picture and a dictated description. Then tie the album pages together with yarn or mount them on a bulletin board at children's eye level.

BEGIN

Join a child or small group of children as they examine the pictures, and encourage them to try to figure out who they think is whom. Offer to help them decide by choosing one picture and reading its dictated description. When you finish reading, look carefully at the photo together and talk again about whom it might be. Encourage discussion among the children and accept all their ideas. If a few children disagree, encourage them to explain their ideas and listen to the ideas of others.

Leave the pictures up for several days so everyone has time to examine and discuss them. At that time, write each child's name on an index card. Place the name cards in the pocket-pages on top of the picture descriptions so everyone can see who is whom. Keep the pictures and name cards on display to encourage more discussion.

Remember

■ This activity works best after children have had time to get to know one another and learn one another's names. It may not work as well at the beginning of the year.

■ When you ask children to talk about themselves, many may begin by giving their names. Explain that you don't want to write down names on the cards because you want everyone to guess who's in the picture.

■ This activity may generate lots of discussion about babies, especially if children have or are expecting babies at home. Be prepared to answer questions about how babies start and grow.

BOOKS

These are good books about being a growing child.

• *When You Were a Baby* by Ann Jonas (Greenwillow Books)

• *I Like to Be Little* by Charlotte Zolotow (HarperCollins)

• *You'll Soon Grow Into Them, Titch* by Pat Hutchins (Greenwillow Books)

PROBLEM SOLVING

Setting up for snack or lunch is problem solving for threes.

LET'S SET THE TABLE

Aim: Children will use one-to-one correspondence, matching, counting, and other problem-solving skills to set the table for a shared meal.

Group Size: One to three children.

Materials: Utensils needed to eat a meal, such as forks, spoons, plastic knives, plates, cups, and napkins, for each person in the room.

In Advance: Clean and sanitize the table or tables where you'll be eating. Set one chair for each person around the tables. Invite children to help.

BEGIN

If you don't already have a table-setting routine, consider making one a regular part of your mealtimes. Invite interested children to be the table setters and ask them to wash their hands. Tell them what you'll be eating. (Or, read your menu together if it's posted.) Then talk about what utensils everyone will need on the tables so they can eat these foods. Together, gather your supplies. As you do, encourage children to think about quantities by asking, "How many will you need? Do you have the amount you need?" Then encourage them to begin setting the tables. Help children keep track of which items they've already placed on the tables and which they still need to set out.

Observe how children approach this problem-solving task. Some threes may count and do simple addition to take the number of utensils they need, while others may carry the utensils to the table one at a time and match each directly to one chair. Support children in whichever method they use. When children say they are finished, help them make sure the table has everything needed.

Remember

■ Table setting is a difficult task for some threes. Even after discussion, they might not realize that they've put too few or too many items on the table. Accept children's best efforts, then make adjustments when the group sits down to eat.

■ In addition to providing problem-solving practice, helping to set the table for lunch or snack lets children feel helpful and responsible and enhances self-esteem. Thank children for their help.

■ Family-style dining, when teachers and children sit together and serve themselves, is preferable to more institutional-type meals. Eating family-style offers you great opportunities to talk informally with children and makes meals a more social, enjoyable time.

BOOKS

Here are good books about sharing meals.

- *The Doorbell Rang* by Pat Hutchins (Greenwillow Books)

- *Potluck* by Anne Shelby (Orchard Books)

- *Daddy Makes the Best Spaghetti* by Anna Hines (Houghton Mifflin)

?

PROBLEM SOLVING

Add a new angle to block play with this spatial challenge.

SQUARE PLAY

Aim: Children will use creative-thinking, patterning, visual-spatial, and fine-motor skills to explore the different shapes that can be made with several squares.

Group Size: One or two children.

Materials: About 12 square unit blocks.

BEGIN

Use this activity to add variety to block play or when you notice children experimenting with sliding blocks along the floor. Sit on the floor with one or two children and arrange six to eight blocks in a rectangular shape in front of each child. Now invite them to play a game with you. Ask children how they might be able to rearrange the blocks without lifting them off the floor. Help children discover that they can do this by sliding. Then encourage them to slide the blocks around to create new shapes. You might need to help them get started by asking open-ended questions such as, "Can you make a long shape?" or, "Which block do you want to move first?" When children have rearranged the blocks, invite them to tell you about their new shapes. They might answer, for example, "This shape is long and skinny," or, "This is a train." Accept all descriptions. Then encourage children to invent additional shapes. Observe as they create. Invite

children to describe their shapes and discuss their ideas with you and with one another. Play until children say they are finished.

Play Another Way!

As a variation, place the blocks on their narrower edges, rather than flat on the floor. You might also play this game using square-shaped hollow blocks. Invite children to work together to arrange these heavier blocks into new shapes.

Remember

■ Keep this activity fun and relaxed, and play only as long as children remain interested.

■ It's not important for threes to use mathematically correct terms to name shapes or discuss ideas such as area or perimeter. What is important is that they explore these concepts in concrete ways.

■ Threes who are interested in counting might want to know exactly how many shapes they're making. Support them by keeping a tally sheet as they work.

■ Threes need many, many opportunities to explore freely with blocks. This activity should be a supplement to lots of ongoing, open-ended block play in your room.

BOOKS

Here are books about building and shapes.

• *Shapes, Shapes, Shapes*
by Tana Hoban
(Greenwillow Books)

• *Changes, Changes*
by Pat Hutchins
(Macmillan)

• *Willy and the Cardboard Boxes*
by Lizi Boyd
(Viking Children's Press)

PROBLEM SOLVING

Who wears this hat? Who uses this tool? Invite threes to decide.

HATS AND TOOLS

Aim: Children will practice matching, use social and language skills, and relate objects to their own experiences as they use props in pairs.

Group Size: Six children.

Materials: Hats and corresponding tools to represent particular roles (one hat and one tool for every two children), such as a football helmet and football, a chef's hat and rolling pin, a hard hat and hammer, a top hat and magic wand, a police hat and whistle or badge, and a firefighter's hat and toy fire truck.

GETTING READY
Put the hats and tools in the dramatic-play area for a few days for children to explore freely. On the day you plan to do this activity, place these props in your group-time area or another roomy area.

BEGIN
Gather near the props and invite each child to choose a hat or a tool. Talk together about the props everyone is wearing or holding. Next, encourage children to form pairs by asking the hat-wearers to find partners who have tools that match their hats and asking the tool-holders to find partners wearing hats that match their tools. Accept whatever pairings children make, even if they aren't what you expected. Then ask children to sit on the floor and talk to their partners. Now, invite one pair to describe and demonstrate how they might use their props. You might begin by asking, "Who do you think wears that sort of hat and uses that sort of tool? Can you tell us and show us how to do that job?" Encourage the two children to talk and work together. Ask questions as needed to encourage thinking and language, and support children's interpretations. When each pair finishes, everyone can talk about the props and the ways people use them.

Remember
■ Be sure the hats and tools you choose represent occupations rather than racial or ethnic groups. Offering props that encourage children to pretend to be, for example, Native Americans or people from China encourages stereotyping.

■ Some threes may have little or nothing to say about their props. Ask one or two questions to stimulate thinking and language, but avoid pressuring children to talk more than feels comfortable for them.

■ Some threes may become impatient waiting for their turn to talk. If interruptions occur, assure the interrupter that everyone will get a turn. Then direct your attention back to the speaker.

BOOKS
Have fun with these books about hats.

• *Whose Hat?* by Margaret Miller (Greenwillow Books)

• *Hats, Hats, Hats* by Ann Morris (Scholastic)

• *Jennie's Hat* by Ezra Jack Keats (HarperCollins)

PROBLEM SOLVING

Combine rhythm and rhyme in this group game.

RHYME TIME

Aim: Children will use language and listening skills to create simple rhymes.

Group Size: Four to six children or your whole group.

Materials: Index cards or paper, a pen or pencil, drawing paper, crayons or markers, and a stapler and staples, or yarn.

In Advance: On an index card or small piece of paper, make a list for yourself of familiar words that can be easily rhymed. Examples might be *cat, blue, red, toy, brown, stand, mad, run, cook, fox, mouse, see, one, way, can,* and *dish.* If possible, include names of people or pets in your program that can be rhymed, too.

BEGIN

Bring your rhyme card to group time. When everyone is gathered together, introduce the Rhyme Time game.

Explain that you'll say a word, then invite a child to think of another word that rhymes with it. First, clap a simple rhythm. Encourage children to join in. Then, while you're clapping, do a "practice round." Decide on a word from your card, choose another adult or a child who is good at rhyming, and, using that person's name, say "When I say 'cat,' Lisa says …" Look at Lisa and invite her to supply a word. Then, repeat the whole chant together: "When I say 'cat,' Lisa says 'hat.'" Now choose a different word and play again. Continue around the group until everyone who wants to has had a turn.

Once children are familiar with the game, add variations. You might invite a child to be the leader and add more complex words as children become more sophisticated rhymers. Also, Rhyme Time is a good game to play at different times throughout the day, such as when you're walking to the playground or waiting for snack.

A Rhyme Time Book Nook

As an extension, read one of Bruce McMillan's books of "terse verse" (see below). Then make a book together. Invite each child to write or dictate a rhyming pair and illustrate it. Use staples or yarn to bind the pages together and add the book to your bookshelves. Later, encourage children to use folded paper and crayons or markers to make their own "terse verse" books.

Remember

■ Although many threes love to play with words and sounds, rhyming can be hard for them. If a child doesn't respond, don't push, but be sure to acknowledge him or her.

■ When asked to rhyme, some children may suggest words that have similar or opposite meanings instead of similar sounds, or make up their own words. Accept these responses. If another child says "that doesn't rhyme," encourage the second child to suggest an alternative.

■ Throughout the year, sing songs, read books, and point out rhymes you hear to help develop children's sense of rhyme.

BOOKS

Add rhyme to your room with these playful stories.

• *One Sun and Play Day* by Bruce McMillan (Holiday and Scholastic)

• *Jamberry* by Bruce Degen (Scholastic)

• *Hop on Pop* by Dr. Seuss (Random House)

PROBLEM SOLVING

Can you guess who is under the blanket?

WHO IS MISSING?

Aim: Children will practice using memory, reasoning, and spatial skills to play a group game.

Group Size: Your whole group.

Materials: A loose-weave blanket or sheet that's large enough to cover a sitting child and light enough to breathe through, and a chair.

In Advance: Place the chair at the edge of your group-time area, facing out.

BEGIN

Gather in your group-time area. Tell children that today you're going to play a game called Who Is Missing? Explain that to play the game, you'll invite one child to sit in the chair you set out and be "it." When "it" isn't looking, you'll pick another child who wants to play and cover that child with a blanket. Then the child who is "it" will turn around and try to figure out who's under the blanket.

Play the game through once so children can see how it works. Choose a child who wants to be "it" and remind him or her not to turn around until you call. Then ask children to raise their hands if they want to hide under the blanket. (Remind children to stay quiet so "it" won't hear.) Quickly choose and cover a volunteer. Then say this chant, using the name of the child who is "it": "Esther, Esther, turn around. One of your friends cannot be found." Repeat the chant a few times and invite children to join in. Then encourage your "it" to look around and try to guess who's missing. If she doesn't know, offer a simple clue, such as the child's hair color, favorite toy, or cubbie location. Invite other children to offer more clues. Once "it" guesses, the child under the blanket can become the next "it." Play the game until everyone who wants to has a turn to hide and be "it."

Remember

■ Being covered with a blanket may frighten some children. Assure them that it's safe, but don't push. Simply let the child rejoin the group and choose someone else who wants to be covered.

■ Often, the missing child throws off the blanket and shouts "It's me!" This is okay — you don't need to play strictly by the rules. After a few games, children will likely remind one another not to tell.

■ This game builds on children's familiarity with one another and their sense of belonging to the group. Play it after you've been together for a few months, when these feelings have had a chance to develop.

BOOKS

Add to the fun by reading these books about hiding and finding.

• *Moongame* by Frank Asch (Simon & Schuster)

• *Hide and Snake* by Keith Baker (Harcourt Brace Jovanovich)

• *Hide and Seek in the Yellow House* by Agatha Rose (Viking)

?

PROBLEM SOLVING

**Here's a great kite —
simple to make and fun to fly!**

CAN A PAPER BAG FLY?

Aim: Children will use creative-thinking, problem-solving, and fine-motor skills to make kites.

Group Size: Four or five children.

Materials: Small paper lunch bags (two per child), yarn or string, masking tape, scissors, a stapler, tissue or streamer paper, crayons and/or markers, other art materials children choose, and a fan (optional).

GETTING READY

On a windy day, gather children together near a large window or outside. Notice the effects the wind has on the environment. Look at tree branches, plants, leaves, clothing, flags, and signs. Ask, "What do you see the wind doing? How can we tell the wind is blowing?" Help children notice that some objects blow in the wind and others do not. Invite them to guess why.

BEGIN

Present a problem for children to help you solve. Ask if they think a paper bag can fly. Offer each child a bag to examine. Take a small group outside while others watch at a window, or use a fan to make "wind" inside. Give children time to experiment with different ways to make their bags fly. Some may throw their bags, fold them, blow them, or even wad them into balls and toss them. Encourage children to open their bags and try to catch the wind inside. Do they feel the air lifting the bag a little? Explain that this is what makes kites fly.

Later, put out new paper bags, tape, a stapler, crayons, markers, tissue strips or streamer paper, and other art materials children choose. Watch as they decorate their bags in their own ways. As each child finishes his or her kite, attach a five-inch piece of string to each of the four corners. Then tie the loose ends of the string together and add a three- to five-foot piece of string for children to hold while they fly their kites.

It's Time to Fly!

Hold the string of your kite up high and demonstrate how to run with it so the wind fills the bag and lifts it. Encourage children to run in different directions and hold their hands at various heights. You can recite this poem by Christina G. Rossetti while children fly their kites.

Who has seen the wind?
Neither I nor you.
But when the leaves hang trembling,
The wind is passing through.
Who has seen the wind?
Neither you nor I.
But when the trees bow down their heads,
The wind is passing by.

Remember

■ Some children may want to try different ways of tying the strings to their kites. Encourage them to experiment. If their ideas don't work, they can always try again, or even choose to make new kites.

BOOKS

| Here are a few books to add to your discussions about the wind. | • *When the Wind Stops* by Charlotte Zolotow (Abelard-Schuman) | • *Fish in the Air* by Kurt Weise (Viking) | • *The Wind Blew* by Pat Hutchins (Macmillan) |

PROBLEM SOLVING

How can water make things look bigger? Find out with these fun experiments.

MAGNIFIER MAGIC

Aim: Children will use the problem-solving skills of experimentation and prediction as they learn about magnification.

Group Size: Four children.

Materials: An assortment of unbreakable magnifying glasses; an empty water table or a few basins; watering cans or small containers filled about halfway with water; self-seal plastic bags; and small objects such as pennies, feathers, marbles, and shells.

GETTING READY

Help your children learn about magnifying. Bring a few small, unbreakable magnifiers to group time. Talk about what they are and how they might be used. Pass around the magnifiers and a few small objects, such as pennies or feathers, so each child can see how much bigger the objects look. Continue experimenting with the magnifiers. Look at other small objects, your skin and hair, or the person sitting next to you. Talk about how the magnifier makes these things look different. Does it let you see things you couldn't see before? Next, ask children to walk around the room and observe other objects through the magnifiers. Invite them to bring objects back to the group area to share.

BEGIN

Water is an excellent magnifier. Let children discover this themselves with the following problem-solving activity. In your empty water table or in basins on your discovery table, set out the watering cans or small containers, self-seal plastic bags, and small objects. Talk about the materials and ask children what they might do with them. Then encourage them to experiment. (Children might like to wear smocks.)

As children play, talk about what they see. Then ask, "How can you use the plastic bags and water to make objects look bigger?" Encourage them to try out their ideas. See if children discover that by filling the plastic bags with water and looking through them at objects, they can create a magnifying effect. Can they find other ways to make objects

look bigger? Ask open-ended questions to guide them, if needed. Allow children to continue playing as long as they're interested. Encourage them to experiment with the water and objects, and observe what happens.

Remember

■ Some children may want to experiment further to find out what would happen if soap or food coloring were added to the water, or to test out other ideas. Facilitate their interests as much as possible by supplying materials and time to experiment.

■ This activity works best near a water source, so children can get more water if they choose.

■ To make cleanup easier, keep towels and a child-sized mop near the table. Be sure to involve children in cleanup.

BOOKS

These books are excellent for introducing the concept of magnification to children.

• *Take Another Look* by E. Carini (Prentice-Hall)

• *What Is It? A Book of Photographic Puzzlers* by Joan Loss (Doubleday)

• *The Wonderful Looking-Through Glass* by Moe Freeman (Scholastic)

? PROBLEM SOLVING

They pop, they fly, where will they land? Have fun predicting the answers.

POPCORN PREDICTIONS

Aim: Children will use observation, comparison, and prediction skills while preparing popcorn.

Group Size: Four or five children.

Materials: Popcorn kernels, a popcorn popper (oil or hot air), one or two large sheets of mural paper, crayons, markers, and experience-chart paper (optional).

GETTING READY

Brainstorm a list of all the things children know about popcorn. Include descriptive words, ways to use popcorn, and where it comes from. Pass around both popped and unpopped kernels to aid in the discussion. You might record the list on experience-chart paper.

BEGIN

Talk about predictions. Explain that a prediction is like a guess. For example, the weather reporters on radio and television make predictions about what the weather will be like tomorrow. Invite children to give other examples of predictions. Explain that today you'll be making a prediction about popcorn.

Begin by placing a large sheet of clean mural paper on the floor. Put the popcorn popper in the center of the paper. *(For safety purposes, leave about four to five feet of exposed paper on all sides of the popper.)* Gather in a circle around the outside of the paper. Explain that today you are going to pop the popcorn without a lid on the popper! Ask children what they think will happen to the popcorn when the lid is kept off. Then ask your prediction question: "How far do you think the popcorn will jump out of the popper?"

Using a crayon, draw a circle on the paper surrounding the popper where you think most of the popcorn will land. Then ask each child to draw a small circle to represent his or her prediction. Help children write their names or initials by their circles.

Now it's time to pop the popcorn! Remind children to stand back because the kernels are very hot as they pop. Have fun as you observe how close the predictions are. After the popcorn has popped, collect it and make another batch (this time with the lid on!) for snack.

It's Raining Popcorn

After snack, begin a discussion based on this fanciful question: "What would happen if the popcorn kept on popping and popping and showed no signs of stopping?" Gather in a circle and record the story on experience-chart paper. Provide markers for children to illustrate the tale. You might feature the story and illustrations in a display entitled "It's Raining Popcorn."

Remember

■ Don't fill the popper with as many kernels as you normally would. One half the amount will still be fun, and you won't have to wait as long to make sure all the kernels have popped.

BOOKS

Here are good books about popcorn to add to your discussions. Set them up in your science center.

- *Popcorn* by Millicent Selsam (William Morrow & Co.)
- *Mr. Picklepaw's Popcorn* by Ruth Adams (Lothrop, Lee & Shepard)
- *The Popcorn Book* by Tomie de Paola (Holiday House)

?

PROBLEM SOLVING

Your room becomes an inventor's workshop as children design and create their own machines.

MAKE AN INVENTION

Aim: Children will use creative-expression, problem-solving, and decision-making skills to design their own inventions.

Group Size: Four to six children.

Materials: Paper plates; pieces of corrugated cardboard or plastic-foam trays; white glue; brass fasteners; pipe cleaners; scissors; markers; tape; construction paper; tissue paper; a variety of scrap materials such as empty boxes, plastic coffee-can and margarine-container lids, and pieces of aluminum foil; and pictures of unusual vehicles and machines from magazines.

GETTING READY

Ask children if they've ever heard of an inventor. What do inventors do? Talk about how inventors make and design things that never existed before. Usually, they are items that help people do things more easily, such as get from one place to another. Explain that people didn't always have cars, airplanes, vacuum cleaners, etc., to help them. Somebody had to invent these machines. Ask, "Can you think of some other machines people invented?"

BEGIN

Children can be inventors, too! Gather together and ask if they have ever imagined inventing a machine that would do what they wanted it to. What would they make the invention do? How would it help them? Talk about problems that could be solved by inventing a new machine. Can they make a machine that flies and cleans house at the same time? How about a vehicle to use in an ice storm? If possible, show children pictures of some new inventions to help spark ideas, such as space modules, land/water vehicles, and Velcro. Talk about other possibilities.

Now, let each child choose a piece of corrugated cardboard or plastic-foam tray as a base to work from. Display scrap materials on a separate table so children have an uncluttered work space. Allow children to use the materials freely as they create. Encourage them to experiment with ways of holding pieces together using glue, pipe cleaners, or fasteners. (You might need to demonstrate how to use a few.) Use other materials such as aluminum foil and tissue paper for decorations.

Have an Inventions Show

After the new machines are dry, ask each child to tell you about his or her invention. Talk about what it does, how it moves, and how it can help the child. Does the invention have a name? Help children to write or dictate stories to display with their machines in a "Great Inventions" show. Invite parents to view the inventions.

Remember

■ Allow children as much freedom as possible. Try to supply additional materials that they might need.

BOOKS

These stories may inspire your young inventors.

• *Mike Mulligan and His Steam Engine* by Virginia Burton (Houghton Mifflin)

• *Good Junk* by Judith Enderle (Elsevier/Nelson Books)

• *Thruway* by Anne and Harlow Rockwell (Macmillan)

? PROBLEM SOLVING

Inspire fours to think creatively when they paint on a variety of unusual surfaces.

HAVE A PAINTING PARTY!

Aim: Children will use creative-thinking, artistic, and fine-motor skills as they experiment with painting on different surfaces.

Group Size: Four or five children at a time.

Materials: A good variety of tempera-paint colors (try mixing some of the basics together to create new shades and hues); many sizes of paintbrushes; a large selection of unusual surfaces to paint on, such as shelving paper, adding-machine tape, computer paper, paper plates, wallpaper scraps, sandpaper, small and large boxes, newspaper, junk materials, egg cartons, paper bags, and nature materials such as dried branches, pinecones, and large leaves; and plenty of newspaper to protect your setting.

GETTING READY

Talk about painting. What do people usually paint on? Where do you usually paint? What other things could you paint on? Ask children to make suggestions. Explain that you are going to have a group paint party. There will be different areas set

up around the room where they can go to paint on some unusual things. "Let's see what kind of special paintings we can make!"

BEGIN

You'll need to organize the event. With children, plan appropriate places for painting "stations." These can be on worktables, at the easel, on top of the sandbox, inside an empty water table, in the block area, or even in the dramatic-play area. Try using a low wall or a hallway to lay out long or big surfaces to paint. Then, together, decide which items to use in the stations. Group similar types of surfaces together. For example, the block area might be a good place for painting on boxes; the easel can hold unusual flat surfaces such as sandpaper, wallpaper, and newspaper.

Once the scene is set, it's time to start the fun. Allow children to choose a paint station and encourage them to create their own masterpieces. Children will want to try different centers and may want to combine their painted objects into one special work of art.

Add Variety

Besides the usual brushes, put out things like marbles, yarn, plastic-foam pieces, sponges, dish mops, natural branches, roll-on bottles, etc. Each of these items inspires the user to figure out different ways to stroke, print, and place the paint on the surfaces.

Remember

■ The process in this activity is much more important than the product. Fours enjoy the challenge of using materials more than thinking about what the outcome will be. Be sure children understand that you do not have any specific expectations so they can feel free to create!

■ Invite family members to join in the paint party. This is a wonderful opportunity for them to see children using their creativity in an open-ended project. They'll probably enjoy the painting, too!

BOOKS

Here are some fun books about painting.

• *Begin at the Beginning* by Amy Schwartz (Harper & Row)

• *Francie's Paper Puppy* by Achim Broger and Michelle Sambin (Picture Book Studio)

• *The Painted Tale* by Kate Canning (Barron's Educational Books)

PROBLEM SOLVING

Fours work together to create a class "flip book" that everyone can enjoy.

CREATE A CLASSROOM FLIP BOOK

Aim: Children will use expressive-language and creative-thinking skills as they create and "read" their own book.

Group Size: Three or four children.

Materials: Crayons and markers, scissors, magazines, heavy white drawing paper cut into 6- by 10-inch pieces, a strong stapler, and a 2- by 1-foot strip of heavy cardboard.

GETTING READY

Introduce the concept of flip books by using one of those listed at the end of this activity or by making one yourself. Show children that a flip book is made up of stacks of pictures placed in a row. The pictures can be "flipped up" and looked at in any order. There are no words in a flip book, so people can create their own stories based on the pictures. "Read" a flip book as a group to help children become familiar with the concept.

BEGIN

Talk about the types of pictures found in flip books. Most pictures are of people, animals, and familiar objects. Ask children to take a few pieces of heavy drawing paper and draw an animal, a person, or an object on each one. Or, they might cut pictures from magazines and paste one on each piece of paper. (If the animal or person is doing something, there is more for the child to talk about.)

Encourage children to talk about what is happening in each of their pictures. After the pictures have been drawn or cut out, randomly place four of them in a row and invite the children to tell a story about them. Place new pictures on top of the old ones and encourage children to continue their story.

Put It Together

Help children group all the finished pictures together in four equal piles. Then place each of the four piles in a row on the strip of cardboard. Staple each pile at the top so the reader can easily "flip" to any of the pictures in the stack. If desired, staple a long piece of paper at the top to form a cover.

Together, decide on a title for your book.

Bring the finished product to storytime and share it with children. Invite those who are interested to come up, one at a time, and use the pictures from left to right to make up a story. Show them how to flip up as many pictures as they want so each time they "read" it, their story is different. Children might like to write, dictate, or tape-record their stories as well.

Remember

■ Flip books and other wordless books are great ways to use literature to practice problem solving. Encourage children to incorporate the pictures they see into their stories. If they choose, they can also add parts that aren't pictured.

BOOKS

| Here are a few flip books and wordless books to show to children. | • *In the Town, Create a Story* (Kiddicraft) | • *Creepy Castle* by John Goodall (Atheneum) | • *The Ballooning Adventures of Paddy Pork* by John Goodall (Harcourt Brace Jovanovich) |

PROBLEM SOLVING

Paper bags, problem solving, and imagination can bring favorite story characters to life.

CREATE A COSTUME

Aim: Children will practice creative thinking and self-expression as they design bag costumes to represent favorite book characters.

Group Size: Four to six children.

Materials: Large paper shopping bags with attached paper or plastic handles (at least one for each child); additional paper shopping bags to use as masks; a wide variety of children's books; experience-chart paper and a marker; an unbreakable mirror; a variety of materials such as juice cans, egg cartons, plastic-foam pieces, empty boxes, fabric scraps, and straw; scissors; glue; tape; crayons; and paint.

In Advance: Cut off the bottoms of the bags that have attached handles. Children can wear the bags as costumes by stepping in and using the attached plastic or paper handles as shoulder straps. (If necessary, you can attach the straps yourself using a stapler and heavy paper.) On the day you begin the activity, arrange the collage and scrap materials on one table so children can easily see and choose items. Set up another table as a work area.

GETTING READY

Bring a few of children's favorite books to group time. Together, brainstorm a list of other books children have read in school, at home, or in libraries. Talk about the characters in the stories. Which do children like best? Ask each child to name his or her favorite character, and write their choices next to their names on experience-chart paper.

BEGIN

Invite children to join you at the tables to make costumes of their favorite characters. Let everyone choose a shopping bag, try it on, and look in a mirror to make sure it fits. Talk again about what characters children want to be. (Some might have changed their minds.) Ask children to look over the collage and scrap materials. Encourage them to use planning and problem-solving skills to decide what types of costumes they want to make. How can they use the materials to represent their ideas? Ask them to let you know if they want other materials, and plan together where and how you'll get them. Then observe as children work. Help those who want to make paper-bag masks cut holes for their eyes, noses, and mouths.

Later, plan an event together in which children can wear their costumes. You might have a Favorite Character party or a parade. Or, children might pretend to be their characters in stories. Encourage them to act out favorite books or invent a few stories of their own.

Remember

■ This is a good activity to extend over several days. The extra time will give children more opportunities to think, plan, and problem-solve.

■ Some children will likely want to create costumes for characters you might consider objectionable, such as Ninja Turtles. Decide ahead of time what your policy will be, and be consistent. Some teachers feel these characters are inappropriate and do not belong in early childhood programs. Others believe that it is important for children to be able to make unrestrained choices.

BOOKS

These books include some all-time favorite characters.

- *Caps for Sale* by Esphyr Slobodkina (Harper & Row)

- *The Giving Tree* by Shel Silverstein (Harper & Row)

- *Corduroy* by Don Freeman (Penguin)

You never know what might spark a creative idea!

IMPROVISE!

Aim: Your children will use creative dramatics and thinking skills as they incorporate a variety of objects into their play.

Group Size: Three to five children at a time.

Materials: It is important to choose a variety of objects, both familiar and not so familiar, for children to experiment with — objects that are not related and can be used in a number of ways. Some examples are: a backpack, many bedsheets, artificial flowers, a clipboard (with paper and pencil), large pieces of beautiful fabric scraps, a toolbox (with some safe but unusual tools), a variety of different-sized boxes, a collection of magazines, and many lengths of rope.

GETTING READY

Start with a creative brainstorming activity. Show an object

and ask children to suggest all the ways it could be used. Choose something that is either unfamiliar or has multiple uses, like a "bungee cord" or even a piece of rope. At first, children will suggest common uses and then, when those are exhausted, they'll think of more unusual ones. For example, a child once said that a short piece of rope could be used as a "jump rope for a cricket"!

Support everyone's ideas with equal excitement. If children get stuck, try suggesting a few funny ideas. When they see that this is acceptable, they'll become more free with their own creative thoughts.

BEGIN

Most of the suggested props work best when introduced one at a time. Then after they have been in the dramatic-play center for a while, add new ones. You'll need to decide when to add by keeping an eye on play. For example, children may have been using the bedsheets for tents and table covers. With the addition of the fabric scraps, they can expand their use of different materials, perhaps into clothing for themselves and the dolls.

You can either leave new props in the dramatic-play area for children to discover or present them to a small group, saying, "Look, I found some new things we can use in the dramatic-play center. I wonder what fun ways you can use them." Then give them the props and allow children plenty of time and space to create with them. Don't try to engage them in a conversation about how they will use them. Just let them go to it on their own. You will be impressed with the results!

Remember

■ Four-year-olds are great creative thinkers, yet they may often adopt an idea a teacher suggests because they think it is "right." Therefore, it is essential to let children spontaneously use these props without any adult direction.

■ Encourage children's ideas for dramatic-play props. They can use materials from your setting or bring in objects from home.

BOOKS

Here are some creative books to add to your read-aloud sessions.

• *I Wish I Had a Computer That Makes Waffles* by Fitzhugh Dodson (Oak Tree Publications)

• *Oh, Were They Ever Happy* by Pete Spier (Doubleday)

• *The Bear's Toothache* by David McPhail (Little, Brown)

? PROBLEM SOLVING

This is a fine tangle to get into — and to find your way out of.

A FRIENDLY WEB

Aim: Children will communicate, cooperate, problem-solve, and have fun as they create and unravel a human "web."

Group Size: Six to eight children or your whole group.

Materials: A very large ball of thick yarn or smooth rope, peaceful instrumental music, and a record or tape player.

GETTING READY

Gather your whole group in a large space and sit in a circle. Put on peaceful music and explain and demonstrate this game: To start, one child wraps an end of a ball of yarn around his or her waist. Then he passes the ball to the child sitting next to him. The second child repeats the action, until everyone is "woven" into one giant circle. When the whole group is connected, stand and move slowly around the circle to the music. When you are finished, help children unwind the yarn.

BEGIN

This version of the game has a problem-solving twist. Another day, put on your quiet music. This time, ask the first child to wrap the ball of yarn around himself. Then, instead of passing it, he rolls it across the circle to another child. The second child wraps the yarn and then rolls the ball across the circle again. The end result is a "web" connecting all the children in the circle.

Now stand and have fun moving together to the music for a while. Then cooperate to figure out how everyone can help unravel the web. One way is to reverse your "weaving" process, so the last child to join the web is the first to unwind from it. Emphasize that children need to talk to one another and work together to untangle the web. End the game by moving freely to the music as "unconnected" individuals.

Remember

■ You might want to start the Friendly Web game with a small group of children. Then, when everyone is familiar with it, try it with your whole group.

■ When you dance in the web, remind children to move slowly so the yarn doesn't pull tightly around anyone's middle.

■ Some children may solve the problem by simply stepping out of the yarn and leaving the web. Accept this solution and encourage the child to stay involved by asking, "How can you help other children unravel the web?"

BOOKS

These resources offer more cooperative game ideas.

• *The Cooperative Sports and Games Book* and *The 2nd Cooperative Sports and Games Book* by T. Orlick (Pantheon)

• *More New Games* by A. Fleugelman (Doubleday)

• *Learning Through Non-Competitive Activities and Play* by B. Michaelis (Learning Handbooks)

PROBLEM SOLVING

Children design their own ways to measure in this end-of-the-year activity.

AS BIG AS ME!

Aim: Children will practice measuring, observing, comparing, and problem solving.
Group Size: Three or four children.
Materials: Yarn, plain white paper, crayons, and scissors.

GETTING READY

Talk about growing by discussing the different ways children have grown this year and the kinds of growing changes they have noticed. Ask, "How many of you have outgrown some of your clothes? Are you the same size as when you started school this year?" If you took measurements at the beginning of the year, compare them to the children's measurements now. Encourage children to bring in clothes or shoes that are now too small for them and compare them to their present sizes.

Another time, on a sunny day, go outside and ask, "What else grows like you?" Look for signs of growth in plants and trees in your area. (New growth appears as the light area of bright green on the ends of branches and plants.) Use pieces of yarn to measure how much the plants have grown. Ask children to look for the plant that has the most new growth on it.

BEGIN

Gather together and talk about times children have been measured, such as at the doctor's office. Ask, "How could you find out how tall you are if you didn't have a ruler?" Encourage children to list all the ways they can think of, such as standing back-to-back with another child or asking someone to mark their height on a doorway.

Now help children separate into pairs. Offer each pair two long pieces of yarn. Talk about how children might use the yarn to help measure one another's heights. One way is for one child to lie down on a clean area while his or her partner stretches the yarn to measure his length. Then the children can trade places. (You may need to help children cut the yarn.) Can children think of other ways to measure their height? Can they make or build things as tall as they are?

What other materials might they use? Encourage children to test out their ideas.

Next, during an outside time, invite pairs to search the playground together as "measuring teams," measuring other objects using their pieces of yarn. Can they find things on the playground that are bigger than they are? Smaller? The same size? At the end of your outdoor time, ask partners to show the group the objects they found.

How Many "Feet" Long?

As an extension, offer children plain paper and scissors to make and cut out a tracing of one of their feet. Then ask them to look at various objects in the play area. Ask, "How can you use this to measure?" Encourage children to see how many "feet" objects are.

Remember

■ Growth is usually a fascinating topic to young children! Consider making this activity part of a theme. You could look together at plant and animal growth as well as children's growth. Seek out ways to include problem solving in your investigations.

BOOKS

Use these books as discussion starters about growth and growing up.

• *Bigger and Smaller*
by Robert Froman
(Thomas Y. Crowell)

• *Blue Sea*
by Robert Kalan
(Greenwillow Books)

• *The Growing Story*
by Robert Krauss
(Harper & Row)

PROBLEM SOLVING

**What makes ice melt fastest?
Experiment and see!**

ICE, WATER, AND SALT

Aim: Children will use the science-process skills of prediction, experimentation, and observation as they examine different ways to melt ice.

Group Size: Four or five children at a time.

Materials: Paper cups, water, table salt or rock salt (if available), three aluminum pie plates, experience-chart paper, and markers. Optional: egg timers, unbreakable thermometers, and unbreakable magnifying glasses.

In Advance: Make a predictions chart. Across the top, write, "Which will melt ice fastest?" Make three columns and use pictures and words to label them for the three methods children will use to melt ice: water, salt, and water mixed with salt. In each column make two boxes. Label one box "predictions" and add a question mark as a visual cue for children. Label the other box "results" and cue it with an exclamation point. Then fill three aluminum pie plates with water and freeze them overnight.

GETTING READY

Talk about ice and melting. If you live in an area where there are winter storms, talk about the different methods people use to melt ice on roads and sidewalks. In warmer climates, children may have noticed ice cubes melting in beverages or ice coolers.

BEGIN

Take out your predictions chart. Together, fill one paper cup with cool water and another with table salt or rock salt. In a third cup, mix water and about one tablespoon of salt. Talk about which of these materials children think will melt ice fastest. Then invite them to show their predictions by marking the numbers *1, 2,* and *3* on the chart in the order they think the methods will melt the ice.

Next, take out the three pie plates filled with ice. Use one plate to try each melting method and encourage children to observe the effects. You might ask, "What do you notice happening to the ice? How do the different plates of ice look the same or different? Do the salt and water melt the ice in

different ways?" Keep watching to see which makes a hole in the ice first, which one second, and which one third. Fill in the results on your chart and compare to your predictions.

Add Variations

Try new comparisons based on children's interests. For example, you might talk about the temperature of the water you used. Was it cold or hot? Do children think using hot water would make the ice melt faster? Test it out and see. Or, if the weather is cold enough in your area, pour some water on the ground in a safe spot and put a few more water-filled pie plates in the freezer. Add salt and/or water and see if the ice melts faster outside or inside. Why? Try setting out timers, thermometers, and magnifying glasses for children to use in their experiments.

Remember

■ Predicting is a form of problem solving. But fives will probably not have a great deal of background information about melting, so don't expect their predictions to be accurate. Discourage competition about who was "right." Emphasize that it's more important for children to gain information as they experiment and observe.

BOOKS

These books talk about changes in temperature and weather.

• *When Will It Snow?* by Syd Hoff (Harper & Row)

• *Seasons* by John Burningham (Bobbs-Merrill)

• *Ice Is ... Whee!* by Carol Greene (Children's Press)

? PROBLEM SOLVING

Use fives' natural interest in bubbles to create a scientific problem to solve.

HOW MANY WAYS CAN YOU MAKE BUBBLES?

Aim: Children use observation, experimentation, and problem-solving skills to create bubbles.

Group Size: Three or four children at a time.

Materials: A bottle of commercial bubble solution and a few blowing wands; dishpans, plastic containers, baking pans, or basins (at least one for each child); a few pitchers for water; a few spoons and a wire whisk for mixing; a variety of detergents and soaps, including liquid, dry, and bar; and glycerin.

In Advance: Set out the materials in your science area or on a water table or any low table in an uncarpeted area. Keep towels and a mop nearby for easy cleanup.

GETTING READY

Bring in a bottle of bubble solution and a few wands and invite children to have fun blowing bubbles. After the initial excitement, guide children's attention to observing the bubbles. You might say, "Let's see what the bubbles do when you blow them through the wand. What do you notice about their shapes, colors, and sizes? What else can you say about the bubbles?" Encourage children to describe what they see.

BEGIN

Gather near the table you prepared and talk about the "science" of bubbles. You might ask, "What do you think this bubble solution is made of? How can we make our own bubble solution?" Ask children to remember times they made bubbles washing their hands or taking a bath. What made those bubbles?

Next, show children the detergents and soaps you collected and invite them to begin creating their own mixtures. Suggest that they pour water from the pitchers into their dishpans. As children experiment, take out the bubble solution you used earlier and invite them to look at and feel it. Fives can use this information to help decide how they want their own mixtures to look and feel.

Invite children to try blowing bubbles with their mixtures

as they experiment. If they aren't satisfied with the results, encourage them to think about what they can add to make the mixture better. Ask open-ended questions to help them consider the possibilities. For example, comparing bubbles made with dry detergent, liquid detergent, and bar soap might help children decide on strategies to try.

After children have had time to experiment and make discoveries, you might want to bring out the "secret ingredient" — glycerin. A few drops of glycerin will make bubble solutions thicker and the bubbles more elastic. Talk about how the mixtures change when glycerin is added.

Remember

■ This needs to be a period of real scientific exploration, so leave plenty of time. Your role is to ask open-ended questions, provide the materials, and let children problem-solve freely.

BOOKS

Here are books about bubbles for children and teachers.

• *Bubbles* by Muriel Rukeyser (Harcourt Brace Jovanovich)

• *Bubbles, A Children's Museum Activity Book* by Bernie Zubrowski (Little, Brown)

• *Investigating Science With Young Children* by R. Althouse (Teachers College Press)

? PROBLEM SOLVING

Inspire your fives to solve building problems.

EXPERIMENTING WITH BLOCK TOWERS

Aim: Children will use creative-thinking, problem-solving, and large-motor skills as they try different methods of building block towers.

Group Size: Three or four children at a time.

Materials: Unit blocks; pictures of skyscrapers, towers, and other tall buildings; and adding-machine tape.

GETTING READY

Begin by having a discussion about the ways people build things. You might ask, "What do you think builders have to think about before they can build a tower?" Explain that when people get ready to build, they experiment to find the best materials and type of construction for the kind of building they want to make. For example, tall buildings, like towers, need a sturdy construction so they won't fall down. Show pictures of different types of buildings to aid in your discussion. If possible, invite an engineer or builder to talk with your group about the problem solving they do when building.

BEGIN

Invite children to pretend to be builders who want to build the highest towers they can, using blocks. Add a dramatic-play element by providing child-sized hard hats or improvising hats using bicycle helmets or plastic bowls. Encourage each child to select one size of block for his or her building. Allow them to build in any way they choose. Some children will naturally place the blocks directly on top of one another, while others create more of a lattice effect. Then, through experimentation, they may discover that the lattice style is more stable and can support a higher tower.

Avoid offering answers to solve building difficulties children may have. Instead, help by asking questions that encourage problem solving. You might ask, "Did you try making a different-sized base? What would happen if you made the bottom larger or smaller?" As children build, periodically encourage them to measure the heights of their towers using their own bodies or a strip of adding-machine

tape. Later, experiment with building towers using different sizes of blocks mixed together, or even using found materials.

Remember

■ If children share "hard hats," wash them every day with bleach solution.

■ Some children may get frustrated if they don't feel successful in their experiments. Still, avoid solving problems for them. You might offer to help a child build his tower, but let the child decide how you can help.

■ Children will naturally compare their towers to one another's. Keep their interactions positive by emphasizing the process, not whose tower is "best."

BOOKS

Here are a few interesting books about building.

- *Changes, Changes* by Pat Hutchins (Macmillan)

- *My Hands Can* by Jean Holzenthaler (E.P. Dutton)

- *I Can Build a House* by Shigeo Watanabe (Philomel)

? PROBLEM SOLVING

Help stretch fives' thinking with these sorting games.

CHALLENGE SORTING

Aim: Children will use problem-solving and creative- and critical-thinking skills as they develop many simple to complex ways to sort and classify household items.
Group Size: Four or five children.
Materials: Different types of spoons or keys; a variety of additional items such as kitchen utensils, bolts, screws, and nails; trays, carpet squares, or paper plates; experience-chart paper; and markers and crayons.

GETTING READY

Present a wide variety of one type of item, such as nails or keys, for children to examine freely and discuss. After they've had time to explore, ask, "How many ways can you use this item?" Invite children to brainstorm all the common ways the item is usually used. Then suggest that they think of nontraditional uses — for example, using a spoon to hammer a nail, open a letter, or dig in the sand. Write children's traditional and nontraditional ideas on two experience charts.

BEGIN

Show children the additional items you collected and encourage them to sort the items in many different ways. (Children can use trays, carpet squares, or paper plates to organize their sorting.) Watch to see how children group the objects. Most will probably begin sorting according to appearance, such as by size, shape, or color. When they finish, encourage them to find new ways to sort. Notice whether anyone sorts his or her objects based on their function. Then suggest that everyone try sorting this way. Refer back to your experience charts for ideas.

Next, children can apply their experiences to their environment. Ask them of they'd like to look around the room for other objects to sort, such as pencils, brushes, or crayons.

Consider ending the activity with an art project. You might ask, "How can we use these objects to create something beautiful?" Encourage children to discuss and try out their ideas, then observe their experiments. For example, some children might make rubbings or prints using keys, or hang spoons to create a wind chime.

Remember

■ Notice children's styles as they sort. Who is strictly logical? Who is more imaginative? Your observations will help you learn more about each child's thinking.
■ Sorting by function is more complex than sorting by size, because it's based on abstract — not visible — qualities. Many, but not all, fives will be ready for the challenge.
■ Encourage children to talk about their actions as they sort, to help develop language skills.

BOOKS

These stories show creative ways to use common objects.

• *The Nightgown of the Sullen Moon* by Nancy Willard (Harcourt Brace Jovanovich)

• *Sam and the Saucepan* by Toni Goffe (Creative Edge Books)

• *Cloudy With a Chance of Meatballs* by Judi Barrett (Atheneum)

? PROBLEM SOLVING

Children build an "architect's model" of their own ideal playground or park.

CREATE A FANTASY PLAYGROUND

Aim: Children will use problem-solving, creative- and critical-thinking, and small-motor skills as they design a model playground or park.

Group Size: Three or four children at a time.

Materials: Unit blocks; art materials such as paper, markers, fabric, and aluminum foil; junk materials; and a camera (optional).

GETTING READY

As you talk about ways we all can respect and take care of the earth, invite children to do some problem solving. Ask what they would do to improve your playground or a local park. Visit the area and look for examples of where the earth is or is not being cared for. (If possible, take photos of the area and/or draw a simple map to which you can refer later.) Back in your setting, you might ask, "What do you think should be added to the playground/park? What needs to be taken away? What improvements do you think are necessary?" Record children's suggestions.

BEGIN

Using the photos and/or the map as a guide, invite children to design what they consider an ideal park or playground, using blocks, art materials, and found objects. (They may want to build a model of the park as it looks now and then add and delete items as they create.) Allow plenty of time for children to experiment as they build.

Children may want to refer to their list for ideas. Be available to help them read it. As children work, watch for the appropriate moment to offer additional props, such as toy children and people to play in the park or additional materials to build with.

When children feel their model is completed, encourage the builders to talk about their creation. Invite children to make suggestions for future improvements. Then ask if they would like to dictate a letter to local officials telling them about their ideas for an improved park or playground. If

possible, take pictures of the model to send with the letter. Also, save some pictures and help children record their comments. Make an album to leave near your block corner.

Remember

■ This is a creative experience, not a scientific one. Therefore, it is not important for children to make their model look exactly like the existing playground/park. The idea is to use this as a jumping-off place and let children explore new ideas.

■ Five-year-olds may want to add signs to their model, so you'll need to provide plenty of paper and writing implements. To help, ask children to think of the types of signs they usually see in a playground/park, or signs they would like to see.

■ When you take a trip to your local park or playground, look for structures that provide accessibility for all children. Talk about whether children in wheelchairs could use this area. Consider how you could improve the playground for children with physical disabilities.

BOOKS

Enjoy these books about parks and ecology.

- *The Little Park* by Dale Fife (Albert Whitman)
- *The Mountain* by Peter Parnall (Doubleday)
- *Wilson's World* by Edith T. Hurd (Harper & Row)

PROBLEM SOLVING

Here's a great way to encourage children to experiment with moving in the wind.

WIND DANCING

Aim: Children will use creative expression, movement, and problem-solving skills as they experiment with moving materials in the wind.

Group Size: Five or six children at a time.

Materials: Scrap materials such as crepe-paper strips, ribbon scraps, strips of cloth, adding-machine tape, aluminum foil, scarves, construction paper, paper plates, cut-up plastic six-pack rings, and paper-towel and/or toilet-paper tubes; tape and/or staplers; scissors; string (optional); and movement music such as Hap Palmer's *Moving* or *Pretend* (Education Activities).

GETTING READY

Start this activity on a windy day. Together, look out the window to observe the ways the wind makes things move. Or, if possible, take a walk outside to see and feel the wind at play. Then talk about the wind. You might ask, "Can you see the wind make things dance? How do the things move?" Invite children to create their own dance movements based on what they see. (This works particularly well if children dance outside or can watch the wind from a window.) Now add music. Play a few selections of movement music (see the suggestions above) and ask children to choose the one they think sounds most like the wind. Encourage them to continue their dances.

BEGIN

Now that children are "warmed up," show them the scrap materials you've collected. Encourage children to try twirling the items to see how they move. Take time to examine and discuss them. You might ask, "What materials do you see here? How do they move? Which items would you like to see moving in the wind?" Then invite children to combine the materials to make their own movement props. As children create, play the windy movement music to help inspire their work.

Take It Outdoors

Once their creations are complete, gather together for a trip

outdoors. Ask children to imagine that, when they dance outside, their props will be their partners. Suggest that children watch how the prop moves in the wind, then create movements to go with it. Go outside and let the dances begin!

After a while, encourage children to try different types of movements, such as high on their toes or low near the ground. You might ask, "What happens when you run with your props? When you stand still? When you move slow or fast?" When children become tired of moving, help them use string to tie their props to a tree or your climbing structure and watch them continue to move in the wind. (Don't forget to take them back inside.)

Remember

■ Be sure to join in the dance!

■ Free exploration of materials, movements, and space is the key ingredient to this activity. Avoid giving any directions or evaluating children's work or ideas.

■ Build on this activity over the following days. Provide new materials and music and encourage children to continue adding to their props.

BOOKS

Try a few of these titles.

• *When the Wind Stops* by Charlotte Zolotow (Harper)

• *Fish in the Air* by Kurt Weise (Viking)

• *The Wind Blew* by Pat Hutchins (Macmillan)

Wordless books are wonderful for stimulating language!

IN OUR OWN WORDS

Aim: Children will use creative-thinking and expressive and descriptive language skills as they make and read wordless books.

Group Size: Three or four children.

Materials: Several wordless books (see suggested titles below) and/or handmade books, plus a few "regular" children's books. For handmade books you'll need drawing paper; a long stapler and staples, or a hole punch and string or ribbon; magazines or old children's books; glue sticks; markers and/or crayons; and a camera (optional).

In Advance: To create your own wordless books, collect interesting pictures from magazines or old children's books you would otherwise throw away. As you decide on pictures, make sure they progress in a sequence that inspires a story line. Next, fold sheets of heavy paper in half. Staple them into the form of a book, or punch holes and tie the sheets together. Now glue your pictures on the pages. If you have a camera, try making photographs of an event at school or home and arrange them in sequential order to make a book.

GETTING READY

At group time, show children your wordless books. Point out that these are special books everyone can read. Compare the wordless books to other children's books and talk about how they are different. Add the wordless books to your bookshelf so children can "read" them independently.

BEGIN

Gather a small group of interested children in a cozy spot. Sit together, hold up one wordless book, and slowly and silently turn the pages. (Children might comment or look at the pictures.) Now explain that you're going to look at the book again and this time make up a story using the pictures.

At first, most children will talk about what they actually see on the page. Accept their comments and, at the same time, encourage them to expand their thoughts. You might ask, "What do you think the characters are doing? What do you think they're saying?" After the story is finished, invite a child to choose another wordless book to read together. (Offer children the opportunity to hold the book and turn the pages.) Repeat the activity as long as children remain interested. Consider recording one of the stories on experience-chart paper so children can see their wonderful language written down!

Remember

■ When choosing wordless books, look for clear and engaging pictures that depict an interesting story line. Books with detailed pictures and lots of action are easiest for children to read.

■ Many children enjoy creating their own books. Provide blank books made from folded paper, and when children are done creating, invite your authors to share their stories at group time.

BOOKS

Share these wordless books with your fives.

• *A Boy, a Dog, and a Friend* by Mercer Meyer (Dial Books)

• *Changes, Changes* by Pat Hutchins (Macmillan)

• *Out! Out! Out!* by Martha Alexander (Dial Books)

PROBLEM SOLVING

Use this lively group game to create an original story.

A CREATURE'S MAGIC BAG

Aim: Children will use creative-thinking and language skills as they make a group story and book.

Group Size: Six to eight children.

Materials: Notepaper and pen; a large plastic bag or pillowcase; and props to place in the bag or pillowcase, such as a hat, a big jacket, a "magic" stick, a pot, a large spoon, and a rock.

GETTING READY

Create an imaginary friendly creature with your group. Talk about what this creature looks like, where it lives, and what it likes to do when it's with friends or alone. Be sure to give your creature a name. Then, away from children, write a note from the creature to the group. The note should say something like this: "Dear Friends, Here is my magic bag. It has some of my favorite things in it. It is magic because all the things inside tell a story. I hope these items help you get to know me. Enjoy! Kindest regards, Your Friendly Creature."

BEGIN

Bring the bag filled with props and gather in a cozy spot. Show the bag to children and read the attached note. Then begin your story. Start by saying, "Once upon a time there was a friendly creature …" Pull a prop from the bag and let it inspire a sentence to add to your story. For example, if you pull out a hat, you might say, "It decided to go for a walk to visit its friend the giant." After you complete your portion, pass the bag to the child next to you. Encourage the child to reach inside the bag, choose an item, and use it to continue the story. Make sure the bag (and the story) is passed to each child until it gets back to you. You or a child can add an ending.

Create a Story

Provide children with paper and ask them to write and illustrate their sections of the story. (Some children may want to dictate their story sections for you to write.) As a group, organize the pictures in sequence and bind them together to create a book. Since this activity is done in small groups, you may have several "Creature's Magic Bag" stories. Invite each group of authors to share its version. Talk about how the stories are different and alike.

Remember

■ Fives will vary in their ability and desire to add to the story. If children need help getting started, ask open-ended questions to inspire ideas. Accept whatever contributions children make.

BOOKS

These books offer lots of creative language.

• *Sing a Song of Popcorn,* selected by Beatrice Schenk de Regniers (Scholastic)

• *The Random House Book of Poetry,* selected by Jack Prelutsky (Random House)

• *The Man Who Sang the Sillies* by John Ciardi (Lippincott)

? PROBLEM SOLVING

Watch how a few sheets and scarves can transform children's play themes.

FUN WITH FABRIC

Aim: Children will use creative and problem-solving skills as they design ways to use sheets and scarves in dramatic play.

Group Size: Four or five children at a time.

Materials: At least one or two old sheets, a collection of colorful scarves in different sizes and textures, markers and crayons, collage items, and experience-chart paper.

GETTING READY

At group time, present the sheets and scarves. Talk about the different materials, inviting children to make comparisons. You might ask, "What do you notice about these sheets and scarves? How are they the same and how are they different?" Next, ask children to brainstorm different ways the sheets and scarves could be used. Start the discussion by asking, "How many different ways can you use these in play? Who can show me one way?" You might need to offer an idea of your own to get children started, such as pretending to be a butterfly by using a sheet as a cocoon and the scarves as wings. Remember, your idea isn't meant to be a model for children to copy, but an example to make the activity less abstract.

BEGIN

Now it's time for children to put ideas into action. Encourage a small group to take the sheets and scarves into the dramatic-play area. This is a "hands-off" time for you as children create and problem-solve together. Instead of joining, observe as children test ideas, see how they work, then discuss, modify, and play some more. Watch to see what roles children take on. Does someone take the lead in creative thinking? In negotiating conflicts? Try jotting down a few notes to use later in family conferences. Be sure to leave ample time for the activity, so children can explore all the dimensions of their play.

Leave the materials in the dramatic-play area as long as children remain interested. Over time, they'll probably find favorite ways to use them. When children begin to repeat common themes, invite them to decorate the sheets and scarves (if feasible) to fit their play. Provide a collection of markers, crayons, and collage materials, and watch as children transform objects into houses, boats, capes — whatever they've been involved with.

Remember

■ You might find that many children want to participate, especially after the brainstorming activity builds their interest. Instead of insisting that everyone take short turns, let children know that the new materials will be available for a long time.

■ Try taking the sheets and scarves outside for a change of pace. Later, compare the ways children use the sheets and scarves in the different areas.

BOOKS

Here are books that invite children to use creative-thinking skills.

- *Daydreamers* by Eloise Greenfield (Dial Books)

- *Good Junk* by Judith A. Enderle (Elsevier/Nelson Books)

- *Regards to the Man in the Moon* by Ezra Jack Keats (Four Winds Press)

PROBLEM SOLVING

Who am I? What do I like to do? Children share about themselves in this unique art project.

"ALL ABOUT ME" BOXES

Aim: Children will use creative-thinking and self-expression skills.

Group Size: Four to five children at a time.

Materials: Cardboard shoe or gift boxes; glue; scissors; tape; magazines and catalogs (to cut up); a variety of collage materials including strips of colored construction paper, paper, and crayons or markers; and at least one photograph of every child, or an instant camera.

In Advance: Collect photographs of children, either from home or by taking them yourself. (If you take the pictures, ask children where they would like to have their pictures taken and what they would like to be doing.)

GETTING READY

Start this activity with a discussion about what makes each person special. You might comment on something a child has done or enjoys, or ask everyone to talk about something they like to do, their families, pets, etc. Encourage children to share their thoughts by asking open-ended questions such as, "If you could do anything you wanted this afternoon, what would you do?" "What are some of your favorite things?" "If you could have any animal for a pet, what animal would you choose?" As children talk, share information about yourself, your family, pets, favorite things, and pastimes.

BEGIN

Gather a small group of children together to make "Me" boxes. Look at the photographs you've gathered and encourage children to tell about the pictures they are in. Ask each child to choose a box and glue his or her picture in it. Now invite children to create their "Me" boxes by gluing things they like inside. Offer magazines and/or catalogs for children to look through, explaining that they can cut out pictures of their favorite things and places, use colored paper to represent their favorite colors, and draw pictures or scenes of things they like. Be sure to give children plenty of time to work, letting them create their boxes over a period of days. (Some children may want to bring small items in from home to add to their boxes.) After everyone is finished, take time to look at and talk about one another's creations. Some children may want to dictate information about their boxes for you to record and place nearby. These boxes make a great display to share with parents and other family members.

EXTEND

Encourage children who are particularly involved in this project to use small jewelry gift boxes to make additional compartments. They can paste pictures and/or place items inside the smaller boxes and fit them into the larger one.

Remember

■ Five-year-olds are at a delicate time in terms of their sense of self. Be supportive of their choices and ideas. Encourage individuality, making sure that you don't transfer preconceived ideas about how the boxes should look or what they should contain.

■ If you want to make a "Me" box to show and share with children, be sure it's not out while children are working so it's not used as a model.

BOOKS

Enjoy these books about "being me."

- *All by Myself*
  by Jean Tymms
  (Price, Stern, Sloan)

- *Look at Me*
  by June Goldsborough
  (Western)

- *Quick as a Cricket*
  by Audrey and Don Woods
  (Child's Play)

ACTIVITY PLAN INDEX:
TWOS AND THREES

DEVELOPMENTAL AREAS AND SKILLS ENHANCED	CRITICAL THINKING	CREATIVE THINKING WITH MATERIALS	CREATIVE THINKING WITHOUT MATERIALS	PREDICTING	DECISION MAKING	SOLVING PROBLEMS IN GROUPS	COOPERATING AND SHARING	LANGUAGE DEVELOPMENT	MATH CONCEPTS	SCIENCE CONCEPTS	SELF-EXPRESSION	FINE- AND GROSS-MOTOR SKILLS
2'S ACTIVITY PLANS												
DRY TO WET PAGE 38	■	■		■				■		■		■
WHAT IS SOFT? WHAT IS HARD? PAGE 39	■				■			■		■		■
WHERE DOES IT GO? PAGE 40	■				■		■	■	■		■	
WHAT CAN WE DO? PAGE 41	■	■			■	■	■	■	■		■	■
AN OPEN ART BAR PAGE 42		■						■			■	■
BUILDING SCULPTURES PAGE 43	■	■			■		■		■	■	■	
PICTURE TALK PAGE 44	■		■		■	■		■			■	
NO! PAGE 45	■	■				■	■	■				■
HOW CAN WE SHARE IT? PAGE 46	■		■		■	■	■	■	■		■	■
SHOE MATCHING PAGE 47	■	■			■		■				■	■
3'S ACTIVITY PLANS												
MAKE A BOAT TO FLOAT PAGE 48	■	■		■	■		■	■	■	■	■	■
WHAT MAKES THAT SOUND? PAGE 49	■	■		■	■	■	■	■		■		■
COLOR MIXING PAGE 50	■	■		■	■		■	■		■	■	■
IT'S NO-SCISSORS DAY! PAGE 51	■	■			■	■	■	■			■	■
"WHO IS WHO?" PAGE 52	■				■	■				■		
LET'S SET THE TABLE PAGE 53	■					■	■	■	■			■
SQUARE PLAY PAGE 54	■	■			■		■		■	■	■	■
HATS AND TOOLS PAGE 55	■	■			■	■	■	■			■	■
RHYME TIME PAGE 56	■		■					■			■	■
WHO IS MISSING? PAGE 57	■			■		■		■	■			

ACTIVITY PLAN INDEX:
FOURS AND FIVES

DEVELOPMENTAL AREAS AND SKILLS ENHANCED	CRITICAL THINKING	CREATIVE THINKING WITH MATERIALS	CREATIVE THINKING WITHOUT MATERIALS	PREDICTING	DECISION MAKING	SOLVING PROBLEMS IN GROUPS	COOPERATING AND SHARING	LANGUAGE DEVELOPMENT	MATH CONCEPTS	SCIENCE CONCEPTS	SELF-EXPRESSION	FINE- AND GROSS-MOTOR SKILLS
4'S ACTIVITY PLANS												
CAN A PAPER BAG FLY? PAGE 58	■	■	■	■	■					■	■	■
MAGNIFIER MAGIC PAGE 59	■	■		■		■	■	■		■		■
POPCORN PREDICTIONS PAGE 60	■		■	■				■		■		
MAKE AN INVENTION PAGE 61	■	■	■		■		■	■	■		■	■
HAVE A PAINTING PARTY! PAGE 62	■	■			■	■	■	■			■	■
CREATE A CLASSROOM FLIP BOOK PAGE 63	■	■	■			■	■	■			■	■
CREATE A COSTUME PAGE 64	■	■	■		■		■	■			■	■
IMPROVISE! PAGE 65		■	■		■	■	■	■			■	
A FRIENDLY WEB PAGE 66	■				■		■	■		■	■	■
AS BIG AS ME! PAGE 67	■	■	■			■	■	■	■	■	■	■
5'S ACTIVITY PLANS												
ICE, WATER, AND SALT PAGE 68	■	■	■	■	■			■	■	■		■
HOW MANY WAYS CAN YOU MAKE BUBBLES? PAGE 69	■	■	■	■	■		■	■	■	■	■	■
EXPERIMENTING WITH BLOCK TOWERS PAGE 70	■	■	■	■	■		■	■	■	■		■
CHALLENGE SORTING PAGE 71	■		■	■	■	■	■	■	■	■		■
CREATE A FANTASY PLAYGROUND PAGE 72	■	■		■	■		■	■	■		■	■
WIND DANCING PAGE 73	■	■	■	■			■			■	■	■
IN OUR OWN WORDS PAGE 74	■		■			■	■	■			■	
A CREATURE'S MAGIC BAG PAGE 75	■		■		■		■	■			■	
FUN WITH FABRIC PAGE 76	■	■	■	■	■		■	■			■	■
"ALL ABOUT ME" BOXES PAGE 77		■			■		■	■			■	■

RESOURCES

Use the following resources for more ideas about how to enhance problem-solving experiences in your program. You'll find them in libraries and bookstores, or you can contact the publisher directly for ordering information. Consider sharing resources with other programs, too!

■ *A New Way to Use Your Bean: Developing Thinking Skills in Children*
by Darlene Freeman
[Trillium Press, Unionville, New York; (914) 726-4444]

■ *Before the Basics* and *Don't Move the Muffin Tins*
by Bev Bos
[Turn-the-Page Press, Roseville, California; (916) 444-7933]

■ *Constructive Play: Applying Piaget in the Preschool*
by George Forman and Fleet Hill
[Addison-Wesley, Redding, Massachusetts; (800) 447-2226]

■ *Creative Activities for Young Children*
by Mimi Brodsky Chenfeld
[Harcourt Brace Jovanovich, San Diego, California; (800) 346-8648]

■ *Explorations With Young Children,*
edited by Bank Street College
[Gryphon House, Rainer, Maryland; (800) 638-0928]

■ *Investigating Science With Young Children*
by Rosemary Althouse
[Teachers College Press, New York, New York; (212) 678-3929]

■ *1-2-3 Art*
by Jean Warren
[Warren Publishing, Everett, Washington; (206) 353-3100]

■ *Playful Perception*
by Herbert Leff
[Waterfront Books, Burlington, Vermont; (800) 639-6063]

■ *Please Touch*
by Susan Striker
[Simon & Schuster, New York, New York; (212) 698-7000]

■ *Suppose the Wolf Were an Octopus?*
by Joyce Paster Foley
and Michael T. Bagley
[Trillium Press, Unionville, New York; (914) 726-4444]

■ *The Piaget Handbook for Teachers and Parents*
by Rosemary Peterson
and Victoria Felton-Collins
[Teachers College Press, New York, New York; (212) 678-3929]

■ *Think It Through*
by Martha Hayes and Kathy Faggella
[First Teacher Press, Weston, Massachusetts, (617) 893-7274]

■ *What Will Happen If …?*
by Barbara Sprung, Merle Froschl, and Patricia Campbell
[Educational Equity Concepts, New York, New York; (212) 725-1803]